Parish Path through Lent and Eastertime

Parish Path through Lent and Eastertime

Second Edition

Edited by Mary Ann Simcoe

Contents

Introduction to the Seasons

Gabe Huck

This book about the 40 days of Lent and the 50 days of Eastertime must begin with three days that are part of neither Lent nor Eastertime.

The Vigil

It must begin with the darkness of a Saturday night–Sunday morning. It must begin with the quiet assembling of people in the dark. Maybe there are many people, maybe there are only a few. They come as individuals, couples, families, friends. In the darkness someone lights a fire, and from it a great candle. By the light of that candle a member of the assembly sings a summons to rejoicing: angels, earth, church, all present, rejoice! The singer proclaims that this is our passover: This is the night when the slaves were saved, when fire destroyed the darkness of sin, when Jesus Christ broke death's chains. This night will see evil driven away, the proud humbled, mourners rejoice, hatred take flight and peace settle in.

Then for a long time in this night the assembly listens to what are perhaps its most sacred scriptures. On this one night of all the year the book is opened to its first page. Only on this night may a reader speak and a people hear the words that stand there: "In the beginning . . ." Over and over again come the words which both judge and direct everyday life: "God saw how good it was." And when that page has been read, readers turn to the story of God's promise to Abraham; to the story of how the slaves escaped right through the sea; to the poems of Isaiah where God woos a people "afflicted, storm-battered and unconsoled," and where the penniless are summoned to feast in a kingdom where tables have been turned; to Baruch's summons to search our God's ways for "she has appeared on earth, and moved among us"; to Ezekiel's promise of a new heart; to Paul's absolutely right question: "Are you not aware that we who were baptized into Christ Jesus were baptized into his death?" and, last, to the page of the gospel where the story is told of the empty tomb.

When all these have been heard and reflected on, a chant begins that calls out the names of the ancestors: saints of all times and places summoned to stand with the present generation, to stand around a font full with water. There the elect are left in no doubt about the stakes. Renunciations are asked: whatever the words, these people are saying they will turn away from whole ways of living. One by one they do this, then promise what will bind them to this people, faith in the Creator, the Redeemer, the Holy Spirit.

Then each one is baptized in the water. The point is drowning: "to believe in Christ is to 'be dead and have one's life hid with him in God' (Col 3:3)" (Alexander Schmemann). It has not changed a bit since the fourth century:

> The ones being baptized verily die by a symbol of that death by which the quickener of all died; and they surely live with a type of life without end. Sin and death they put off and cast away in baptism, after the manner of those garments which our Lord departing left in the tomb. As a babe from the midst of the womb they look forth from the water; and instead of garments the priest receives them and embraces them. They resemble babes when they are lifted up from the midst of the water; and as babes everyone embraces and kisses them. Instead of swaddling clothes they cast garments on their limbs, and adorn them as brides and grooms on the day of the marriage supper.

After the waters comes the perfumed oil called chrism, poured on each newly baptized head, sealing the baptism as the sweet odor fills that hall. Then all join in making intercession, bread and wine are brought to the holy table where with prayer and acclamation they are blessed, and after sharing the kiss of peace all eat of the one bread and drink from the cup.

Those deeds are the only beginning this book can have. This night, truly kept by an assembly, is not important because of a few moving ceremonies. Rather, this night matters because we deal most leisurely, most intensely, most completely in the mystery which is our baptized life. What we do this night is, to all appearances, very unworldly: sit in the dark for long readings none of which came into being less than 1,900 years ago, use strange, even foreign words like "renounce" and "alleluia" and "body and blood," gather around a pool of simple water and there immerse or splash the newcomers, then acclaim them, embrace them and anoint them with oil. Who in the world would give up a Saturday night for this?

Yet for those who gather it is the most worldly Saturday night of the year, the night of all nights most about this world. For the life that is affirmed and embraced this night is not merely a life eternal that begins way down the road, an afterlife of bliss. The death which we proclaim defeated is not merely the death that each of us must die. This is a worldly night because what is defeated—so we hear and so we mean, though the news is traveling very slowly—what is defeated is death in life, that death which masquerades as life: the death that dwells in economic and political systems when even the least human being comes in second, the death that dwells in our very selves when we dwell at ease with bounty and allow the balance to grow more and more lopsided while we continue beating our children's world into swords, that death that dwells in homes and nations when we learn and teach that any color is better, any sex, any age, any nationality, any status.

This night we affirm the death of all that death, for we know—just hear those scriptures, just look at that woman entering the waters, just smell that chrism, just taste that wine—we know what is passing away and what abides. This is our passover, that paschal mystery that we proclaim: Dying he destroyed our death, rising he restored our life. The liturgy this night is worldly through and through, just as we are and will be. It is ours. It is what we need, what we undoubtedly cannot do without, if we desire the making of new Christians and the renewing of old Christians.

It is clear that we don't just get up from the dinner table on a Saturday night and stroll over to the church for such a vigil. Nor do we walk out afterwards expecting a typical Sunday. The Vigil can be only within the Triduum, and that can be only when there is a Lent and an Eastertime. But none of these—Triduum, Lent or Eastertime—has any existence apart from people's lives.

The Triduum

We can come to the Vigil, we can do the Vigil, because since Thursday we have been making ourselves ready.

The *Constitution on the Sacred Liturgy* of Vatican II has a remarkable little paragraph: "Let the paschal fast be kept sacred. Let it be celebrated everywhere on Good Friday and, where possible, prolonged throughout Holy Saturday, so that the joys of the Sunday of resurrection may be attained with uplifted and clear mind" (#110).

Take that slowly. This is a "paschal" fast (the lenten fast has ended), a fast which is to be "celebrated" (not just "kept" or "endured"). It sounds like a serious fast, not just a no-eating-between-meals sort of thing, and it sounds this way because of what it is to accomplish: to bring us to the Vigil with "uplifted and clear mind." So it is a fast of excitement like the failure to eat, the loss of appetite, that happens before one gets married. It is a foodless two days so that by Saturday night we have our minds clear, our senses sharp.

Such a fast is truly the ritual keeping of Good Friday and Holy Saturday. It takes things beyond the limits of the liturgies and fills our lives with the holiness of the time. This fast is what any self-respecting tribe would be engaging in before daring to enter into its sacred rites of initiation. Fasting, we can't pretend that the initiating work is up to someone else (the parish staff, the catechumenate team). We know it belongs to all of us. Fasting leads us to the ways that these whole two days are a time to watch and pray.

So it becomes clear that the liturgies of the Triduum are not some effort to gather now and then to remember what was happening to Jesus at this moment. We see instead, that our assembly on Thursday night is for our entrance into the Triduum. In its first moments we proclaim that our *glory* is the *cross*, and throughout the three days we refuse to do anything but bind those two together.

The gesture of Thursday night which makes it clear what sort of church we are is the mandatum, the washing of the feet. Here is the gesture of our service, to kneel down and care for one another. And here too is an image of what is to come at the Vigil; this is how Origen put it: "Wash my feet, then, so that I must be made clean with that other washing of which you said: 'I have a baptism with which I must be baptized.'"

Once we have entered the Triduum on Thursday night, we remain there. The liturgy that night has no dismissal; the liturgy Friday has no entrance and no dismissal. The church is watching and praying.

Through the whole time there are the scriptures. On Thursday we read from Exodus, from 1 Corinthians, from John; on Friday, Isaiah, Hebrews and John's narrative of the passion (where "glory" and "cross" are inseparable). Pondering these texts and others (books like Lamentations and Jonah have a special place in the reading of these days), we keep the hours of Friday and Saturday till we assemble for the Vigil itself.

After the Vigil there is continuing celebration. The breaking of the fast that happens at the Vigil's holy communion continues on Easter morning and day. The Triduum concludes quietly and simply with the newly baptized and their community gathered again at the font on Sunday afternoon for evening prayer.

The Paschal Season

In our present practice, we are coming to see all the days from Ash Wednesday to Pentecost as the paschal (passover) season. The 40 days of Lent and the 50 days of Easter surround the Triduum. The entire season has a unity founded in the Vigil and manifest in the preparation for the sacraments of initiation (Lent), and the continuing celebration of these initiation rites (Eastertime).

Such an understanding of the Lent-Eastertime is not to make too much of some individuals being baptized, confirmed and welcomed in holy communion. It is, rather, to express how these deeds bind the whole community to its God in the paschal mystery of Jesus. Setting aside a night in all the year when this will be done and surrounding that night with days of preparation and days of celebration are our human way of keeping the initiation deeds from becoming theological abstractions. It is a question of how the initiating deeds can center and nourish a community, can in fact and with some regularity bring a community face to face with what it truly became when baptized into Christ Jesus.

The annual rhythm we have inherited for this is quite ancient. In the Northern Hemisphere it corresponds to the waning of winter and the life of springtime. That is no accident. In ancient rites of gratitude for the return of fertility in fields and flocks we find the origin not only of the Jewish Passover's use of unleavened bread and the lamb, but of such things as tokens of life itself. That is the story Passover tells new to each generation—a story of the earth but also of the people, a telling that not only in an ancient generation but in every generation the Lord has seen the oppression of the people and has set about leading them to safety, freedom, solidarity. The very sense for such a passover gave the followers of Jesus a way to speak of and understand what they believed had happened. They spoke of him as "our passover" and they told of his passage, his exodus, in the vocabulary and context of the Passover itself. Just a few generations later, when the growth of their communities brought about a need for order, there gradually came to be this yearly "great Sunday" (bound always to the date of Passover) when the Christian's own passover from death-in-life to life in Christ Jesus took place in the waters of baptism.

In later years, when it had become more customary to baptize infants and when baptism was regarded as more of a washing away of sin than the likeness of our whole life in Christ, the yearly Vigil had nothing to sustain it. The liturgies of Easter and the days before became then something close to a "passion play," an effort to walk with Jesus through his suffering, death and resurrection. This was *capable* sometimes of emotional power, but it could become very private, very independent of the community. And it did. To a great extent, it still is.

Lent in this long era evolved into a time when attention was fixed on Jesus' passion and on penance. It climaxed then in the Good Friday commemoration of the passion and in the Holy Saturday end of penance. Easter Sunday was an anniversary of the resurrection, which was seen as a great miracle. Eastertime as a 50-day season, the year's Sunday, disappeared altogether, leaving only the various Sundays "after Easter."

The liturgical renewal of our time makes it clear that we are set now on a very different course. The dimensions of what is hoped for make it equally clear that many years, many generations perhaps, will be needed before the renewal has its full effect. Central to this renewal are the *Rite of Christian Initiation of Adults* and the reform of the calendar. Together they make it possible for a local church again to make the Vigil the strong initiation deeds of a community. They allow for this community to have prepared itself most immediately with the prayer and paschal fasting of the Triduum, and before that with 40 days of lenten fasting, almsgiving and prayer. All of this takes place around the catechumens who have become the elect and have been the focus of that scrutiny process which Lent is for the whole church. The RCIA and the calendar allow, too, that Easter Sunday to Pentecost is 50 days of rejoicing, of the mystagogia, of the unfolding of the mysteries which we have celebrated and which we are.

The *General Norms for the Liturgical Year and the Calendar*, after dealing with our most basic rhythm of the Sunday and the weekdays, speaks of the rhythm of the year. First consideration is given to the Triduum, then Eastertime, then Lent. The text is important:

> The Easter Triduum of the passion and resurrection of Christ is the culmination of the entire liturgical year. Thus the solemnity of Easter has the same kind of preeminence in the liturgical year that Sunday has in the week. The Easter Triduum begins with the evening Mass of the Lord's Supper, reaches its high point in the Easter Vigil, and closes with evening prayer on Easter Sunday. On Good Friday and, if possible, also on Holy Saturday until the Easter Vigil, the Easter fast is observed everywhere. (#18-20)
>
> The 50 days from Easter Sunday to Pentecost are celebrated in joyful exultation as one feast day, or better as one "great Sunday." These above all others are the days for the singing of the Alleluia. (#22)
>
> Lent is a preparation for the celebration of Easter, for the lenten liturgy disposes both catechumens and the faithful

to celebrate the paschal mystery: catechumens, through the several stages of Christian initiation; the faithful, through reminders of their own baptism and through penitential practices. Lent runs from Ash Wednesday until the Mass of the Lord's Supper exclusive. (#27–28)

Could it be otherwise? Could there be another structure of time so that in some very different rhythm the deeds of initiation might be done, always bound up with the whole community's practice and consciousness? Certainly. This rhythm of the Forty Days, the Three Days, the Fifty Days is a recovery and reform of our tradition. But in other times, places and cultures the church might well seek a very different approach. What is so crucial in the present generation is not that we have recovered *the* way to initate, and so to structure our year. What is crucial is that we have begun to rediscover initiating: that it is always at the center of how this people understands itself, continually reforms itself, and hopes to be in the world.

The RCIA made its entrance over a decade ago, the calendar norms almost two decades ago. Some things have come about in some places. Even so we are very far from grasping the deep implications. The whole paschal season—Ash Wednesday to Pentecost—does not exist in ordos and calendars and sacramentaries. It exists only in churches, people. It cannot be peripheral, merely moving, merely something lovely or dramatic or therapeutic. Far more is at stake. In these days and their initiatory deeds, we face the struggle we plunged into at baptism: struggle that we see and feel with racism, sexism, with the waste of creation on idle goods and arms, with brutal systems of right and left, with the enormity of the separation between rich and poor, powerful and powerless. We discover more deeply each year that the way we have chosen is set against so much of our world. We have a Lent when we gird ourselves and strive to become clear-sighted. We have an Eastertime when we dare act as if God's reign had reordered things here and now. In between these two times, we wash feet, kiss the cross, fast, watch, listen to long scriptures, chant, approach the waters of that womb and tomb, that birth and death place for all of us. All of this is not a code to be translated. It is the emerging shape of our lives. Year after year, it becomes so.

Lent

Such a season clearly means that the community puts aside much of the business that occupies it all year long. We cannot keep Lent unless it is its own space, greatly free of the usual round of activities, free also of the celebrations of those sacraments which come within the Triduum or are more properly celebrated at Eastertime—baptism of infants and adults, confirmation, first communion, weddings, communal anointings. Lent is, of course, much involved with the practice and sacrament of reconciliation.

What then is Lent free *for*? The disciplines of prayer and of fasting and of almsgiving provide today, as before, an ample battleground.

Can there be a church at prayer in Lent when there is not a church that is fasting? Can the words and the gestures—ashes, stories of wilderness and transfiguration and Lazarus, hymns and chants—find any place when life is already full? Are not the liturgies of Lent possible only within a larger ritual structure, a ritual of fasting that brings us to face how much emptiness and how much hunger we have in ourselves? Fasting is discovering our hunger. This discipline is rooted in our bodily hunger, but fasting becomes the metaphor for the whole of church life as its business-as-usual and even sacrament-as-usual is suspended. We fast from these. We try to find what we truly hunger for, what we truly need. Fasting clears the deck, simplifies, frees, shows what a just world would look like, speaks of taking on the suffering of injustice until justice is done.

Almsgiving is but the other face of this. It is to remake the world, or, rather, to restore it. It has to do with time and space, with money and goods. It is about the wholeness of things and people, the right relationships of those who dwell on the earth to the earth and to each other. It aims to right the maldistribution caused by greed or power or whatever else. It ignores neither the world nor what is in front of one's face. Like fasting, almsgiving is a year-round habit, but being who we are, we need a Lent to put ourselves in this shape.

We have these two disciplines—fasting and almsgiving—and, within their practice, we have the prayer of Lent: the Sunday scriptures and eucharist, the practice of daily morning and evening prayer, the daily scriptures. Real fasting and real sharing of time and wealth raise our awareness: we come before the scriptures more alert, the mind and heart somewhat clarified, sharpened, ready to hear. And so we hear the scriptures and the preaching, the songs and prayers, as at no other time. There is something in Lent that not only makes us pay attention but also helps us discover what we must pay attention to. We see and hear more clearly: inside us, at home, in the newspapers, we come to know where our attention belongs.

A great part of this has to do with the troublesome presence of the catechumens. Early in Lent they are enrolled for baptism so that all along we know toward what deed all this lenten discipline is directed. Then Sunday after Sunday they are scrutinized, an icon of what Lent itself is for all of us. And right up until the Vigil they are dismissed to pursue their reflection on scripture while we proceed to do the Sunday eucharist.

Eastertime

On the other side of the Triduum, what do we know of keeping Eastertime? Very little, as yet. We know this: Keeping the Eastertime is nothing but the overflow of the Vigil. There has to be a Vigil (and before it, the preparation of Friday and Saturday, and before that, the Lent itself) for there to be an Eastertime. And it is in the Vigil that we find the spirit of the Fifty Days. The scriptures of the Vigil make us ready to hear the lectionary of Eastertime. The same scriptures give us the great images within which we baptize and confirm and share eucharist on that night, then go on for the Fifty Days to sing and speak of these mysteries, to contemplate in what way we have died and in what we now live.

When the catechumenate flourished in the early church, the Fifty Days were the time when all that had been done at the Vigil's initiation was talked about: the nakedness of the catechumens, the anointing before baptism, as if for a wrestling match, the harsh renunciations and the greeting of peace, the eucharistic feast. These were talked about, not to turn them into an elaborate code, but to open up the ways in which they put the new Christian into the pattern of Christ.

One thing is clear: We cannot talk about it until we have experienced it. First we must so care for and respect the rites, must allow them to be the work of the assembly, work which expresses the people's whole lives. Then we will have something to talk about, the content of our Eastertime. These days, then, become the time when signs of this life abound: in first communions, in confirmations, in weddings, in rites of commissioning and ordination, in the anointing of the sick. These are hardly matters of pretty ceremonies. They are in fact the signs that what we did at the Vigil was true: that God's wisdom has moved among us and "all who cling to her will live," that all who are thirsty may come and drink and those with no money may come and feast, that earth and heaven are wedded. It is that wedding which is kept through these days, kept, of course, despite nearly everything. A wedding means vesture that is special, delight in wine, song and dance, flowers and a sort of quiet extravagance, many sorts of signs and blessings for fertility. All of that so that the future may be embraced with the promises we have made, made in the company of one another.

What becomes so clear is that Lent and Eastertime are not their liturgies. The liturgies are the assembly's ordered gatherings for scripture, reconciliation, eucharist, and other such business of the church. But they can exist only within the ritual that is the people keeping the time itself: the fast, the almsgiving, the individual and household prayer of each day, the good work and the disciplines and the ever-deepening perception that become a way of living from Ash Wednesday to Pentecost.

The liturgies, then, with which this book is concerned, are not approached as so many individual meetings to be planned for people who come in unaware. They are the weekly and the annual assemblies of people who are learning to do what they know deeply how to do, people who are presumed to be making overtures toward keeping Lent and Easter. Those who take responsibility for the liturgy take responsibility for serving this assembly: for seeing that each ministry is humble and accomplished service, for seeing that pace and order and eventual familiarity make this time together seem to be what it is, the work of the people.

The Lectionary

Eugene LaVerdiere

LENT

Lent is a proclamation of Christ's victory over sin and death, a celebration of what God already has accomplished in the Son, and a commitment to pattern our lives on that of Jesus. Lent is a time of repentance and renewal when the church attends to the most basic elements of Christian life.

Today, as in the church's longstanding tradition, the function of Lent is threefold. First, the church prepares the elect for baptism into the Christian community. Second, it wants to move those who already are baptized to renew their commitment to the Christian life and mission. Third, the church examines its life, aims and structures for conformity to the passion and death of Christ. At all three levels, Lent focuses on the perennial need for purification and enlightenment.

To fulfill these functions, the lenten season challenges the church community with a series of liturgies which lead to the celebration of the Triduum and its climax in the Easter Vigil. It is then that the newly baptized are received, that the assembly renews its baptismal pledge to walk in the light of Christ, and that the entire church proclaims Christ's Passover as its own.

Lent is an organic liturgical unit, a synthesis of Christian life, not a mere juxtaposition of weeks of Sundays. From a pastoral point of view, Ash Wednesday can be seen as its introduction and the six Sunday liturgies as complementary celebrations with each Sunday presupposing the others and contributing to the season's function in the liturgical year. Were we to approach these liturgies

12

as distinct and isolated events, our lenten celebration would lose its formative impact and fall far short of its intended purpose.

Consequently, for the church's lenten program of rebirth and renewal to be effective, we must be especially sensitive to the particular function each liturgy plays within the whole. Concretely, this requires careful attention to the liturgies of the word and to their progressive development from the beginning of the season to its climactic celebration. As on all Sundays and feasts, the gospel provides the key liturgical reading, and the other readings, along with the rest of the liturgy of the word, are related to the gospel. Our lenten liturgical preparation and actual celebration must therefore pay special attention to the sequence of lenten Sunday gospels.

The three synoptics set the tone for each of the cycles. In cycle A, Matthew shows us how to celebrate Lent as missionaries whose roots lie in Judaism but who are eager to embark on the Gentile mission. In cycle B, Mark spurs us to renew our gospel commitment to follow Christ, whatever the cost. In cycle C, Luke is our guide for a lenten reconciliation in Jesus, the savior, messiah and Lord of all. All three cycles draw also from John's gospel, which helps us to see the human and physical as signs of the divine and spiritual.

In addition to the biblical context, we must be equally aware of the liturgical setting for our readings. It is not enough to interpret the readings in their ancient biblical framework. We must now see them as related to one another in the liturgy, where their combined message is brought to bear on the eucharistic celebration and proclamation.

In the liturgy, the church brings texts together in a new way. These texts comment on one another and illumine one another, creatively revealing meaning for our time which texts do not have when they are viewed exclusively in their biblical, literary and theological context. This Lent and every Lent, the church provides a liturgical hermeneutic of scripture for Christians confronting the challenges of today.

Ash Wednesday

The liturgical celebration of Ash Wednesday is the same for all three cycles. Like the Sundays of Lent, it includes three readings.

The first reading rends the air like a mighty trumpet blast. With an extraordinary passage from Joel, the church calls for a return to the Lord, proclaims the beginning of a great fast, and announces a season of prayer, repentance and penance (2:12–18). The reading's focus is on the whole assembly. Lent is a communal observance which touches every member of the Christian community.

After a meditative song of repentance (Ps 51:3–4, 5–6, 12–13, 14, 17), the church addresses us in words first spoken by Paul to the church of Corinth (2 Cor 5:20–6:2). In the spirit of the apostolic church, the ambassadors of Christ call us to reconciliation. The time of salvation, announced by Joel, is now.

Matthew provides the gospel text (6:1–6, 16–18). It includes an introductory warning concerning public display in performing religious acts and an application of this general statement to three important areas, giving alms, prayer and fasting. In all three cases, the liturgy warns against hypocritical behavior. Religious acts are performed for a divine reward, not for a human one. Staying close to the ancient oral catechesis, the liturgy omits the gospel's developments on prayer, including the Lord's Prayer (6:7–15), which were added later when the gospel was written down.

The Sundays of Lent

There are six Sundays in Lent. But since Lent comes to its climax and fulfillment in the Easter Triduum and Eastertime itself and is quite meaningless without these, we must keep them in mind when considering the structure of Lent. When we do so, particularly if we focus on the Easter Vigil, it becomes clear that the first two Sundays constitute a twofold introduction which parallels and announces Passion Sunday and Easter, Lent's twofold conclusion. The third, fourth and fifth Sundays of Lent, the season's body, so to speak, apply the paschal mystery to various aspects of Christian life.

Cycle A

In cycle A, the year of Matthew, the gospel readings for the Sundays of Lent are taken from Matthew and John. On the first two

Sundays, we have Matthew's account of Jesus' response to temptation (4:1–11) and of the transfiguration (17:1–9). On the third, fourth and fifth Sundays, we turn to John. Jesus offers new life to a Samaritan woman (4:5–42), gives sight to a man blind from birth (9:1–41), and calls his friend Lazarus from death (11:1–45). On Passion Sunday, we return to Matthew for the procession with palms (21:1–11) and the story of Jesus' passion (26:14–27:66). At the Easter Vigil, the gospel reading is Matthew's account of the women's visit to the tomb of Jesus (28:1–10).

The lenten gospel for cycle A thus begins and ends with Matthew. His accounts of Jesus' victory over temptation and his transfiguration provide Lent with a two-Sunday introduction, which parallels Lent's climax in Jesus' ultimate test and his manifestation as risen Lord.

FIRST SUNDAY

The First Sunday situates us in the primal struggle between good and evil. Jesus is in the desert. After fasting for 40 days, he is hungry. The devil confronts him with humanity's most fundamental test (Mt 4:1–11). Shall he accept the human condition with all its limitations? Shall he accept his creaturely status before God? Jesus' response is clear. Divine sonship does not destroy human limitations, and as a child of earth he must serve the one who formed him from the earth.

The acceptance of humanity's most basic limitation, mortality, is a central theme in the first reading where we hear of the human couple's fatal choice in Eden's garden oasis (Gen 2:7–9; 3:1–7). The temptation is simple: "You shall not die; you shall be like gods, knowing all things." Our lenten challenge is to join Jesus in accepting our humanity and mortality (Rom 5:12–19).

SECOND SUNDAY

Last Sunday's account of the triple temptation emphasized Jesus' humanity. The Second Sunday of Lent focuses on his divine sonship. Having considered Jesus' victory over evil, we rejoice in his transfiguration, a divine manifestation which evokes the great theophanies of the Hebrew Scriptures and announces the Easter experience of the resurrection (Mt 17:1–9). Jesus' face becomes dazzling, his clothing radiant. The cloud of God's presence descends as on Sinai. The Old Testament is present in Moses and Elijah; the New is present in Peter, James and John.

The experience of Jesus' transfiguration is too much for the disciples, and they must not speak of it before the resurrection. Apart from Jesus' rising from the dead, who would understand that the promise of blessing to Abraham was fulfilled in the person of Jesus, God's beloved Son (Gen 12:1-4)? God's gracious design of salvation, manifest in Christ Jesus, leaps across the ages to touch us with life and immortality (2 Tim 1:8-10).

THIRD SUNDAY

With Peter, James and John, we have come down from the mount of transfiguration (Mt 17:1-9). Our hope is secure. We have been given the promise. We know that death has been vanquished, and that life is offered to us. On this Third Sunday of Lent, we take up John 4:5-42 to join Jesus and a woman at a well in Samaria. We learn to appreciate the sacramentality of baptismal water whose life-giving quality transcends nature and sustains us through history. Progressively, our baptismal encounter with Christ enables us to unmask the hypocrisies of life, disentangle its ambiguities, grow in the goodness called for by Christ, and become his witnesses.

Our thirst is not unlike that of the Israelites in their desert wandering. The water which Moses gave, however, provided strength to reach an earthly promised land (Ex 17:3-7). The water which Jesus gives wells up within us to give eternal life in a heavenly land of promise. In that water, touched by faith, the love of God has been poured out in our hearts. Sinners though we were, we have received peace and hope (Rom 5:1-2, 5-8).

FOURTH SUNDAY

At this Sunday's heart is sight and light. Like the thirst-quenching water which Jesus provides (Third Sunday), the sight he grants is associated with baptism. With John 9:1-41, we learn that physical evil is not the result of anyone's sin and that, like the man who was born blind, we must have our eyes opened to see. Just as physical blindness can symbolize a far more profound blindness, physical sight can symbolize the sight of faith. Many who have eyes to see are actually blind. Many whose eyes are unable to see enjoy the sight of faith.

The gospel is a challenge to us. Shall we be like those who were threatened by the new sight of one who had been born blind? Or shall we give glory to God for this gift of sight? Shall we accept to see as God sees? The human eye sees the appearance. God sees into the heart (1 Sam 16:1, 6–7, 10–13). We ourselves were once blind. As we read in Ephesians, we were in darkness. Now that we have faith, we must live as children of light (5:8–14).

FIFTH SUNDAY

On the Third Sunday of Lent, we reflected on the human thirst for eternal life and the water Jesus provides. On the fourth we came face to face with our blindness and welcomed Jesus' gift of sight in faith. Today, in John 11:1–45, we see Christ as the life and the light, the one who invites us to risk death that we might live in the light. Through faith in Jesus, our own life already is eternal. We experience this liturgically in the story of Lazarus, whose death and resurrection prepares us for that of Jesus. Jesus' action on Lazarus' behalf evokes belief in Jesus' divine mission. With Lazarus, we respond to Jesus' freeing call to life.

The first reading holds out the promise of God's life-giving spirit. Though we be dead in our graves, the Lord will open our graves and have us rise from them. He will place his spirit in us and we shall live (Ez 37:12–14). The second reading develops the same theme. It is through sin that we have died in the flesh, but it is through justice that we live in the Spirit of Christ (Rom 8:8–11). The three Sundays that make up the body of Lent have thus led us to Lent's climactic presentation of the passion and resurrection of Jesus.

PASSION SUNDAY

The Procession with Palms

The characteristic gesture of Ash Wednesday is the signing with ashes; that of Passion Sunday, which is still popularly referred to as Palm Sunday, is a procession with palms. It evokes the story of Jesus' solemn entry into Jerusalem. In Matthew 21:1–11, the significance of Jesus' entry on the colt of an ass is extremely clear. The prophetic quotation, which draws from Isaiah 62:11 and Zechariah 9:9 shows Jesus coming in on the work animal of the humble and poor, not astride the horse of a conqueror. The prophet Jesus from

Nazareth is hailed by the crowd as the Son of David, but the Galilean king is like no other—the Lord does not need the trappings of power to reign.

The Liturgy of the Word

The gospel reading is the passion of our Lord Jesus Christ according to Matthew (26:14–27:66). Each of the synoptic accounts of the passion tells how a successful plot to destroy Jesus was transformed by him from a tragedy in which Jesus was executed into a gift of life to others. At the same time, each of the passion accounts is unique. Matthew's account of the passion gives more prominence to Judas than do the others. In his dialogue with Jesus at the supper, the betrayal in the garden, and his clumsy effort to undo the harm he had done, we sense the evil and terror to which all are susceptible. The 30 pieces of silver are an especially powerful Matthean symbol. The death of Jesus is surrounded with extraordinary events not unlike those which accompany a theophany. The curtain of the sanctuary is torn from top to bottom. The earth quakes, tombs are opened and the saints are raised from the dead. There are those who have heard that Jesus' body would be stolen and that his disciples would claim that he had been raised from the dead. A guard was stationed at the tomb.

The first and second readings are the same in all three cycles. With Isaiah we hear the Lord's suffering servant at prayer. He has not turned away from the blows, the buffets and the spitting. The Lord is his help. He is not disgraced (50:4–7). After the servant's song, we meditate with Psalm 22, whose phrases we recognize from the passion narratives. We then move on to the second reading, a christological hymn from Paul's letter to the Philippians. Christ fully accepted to be human and mortal. He reversed humanity's primal sin (see cycle A, First Sunday of Lent). And that is why God exalted him (2:6–11). Passion Sunday anticipates Easter. The passion is meaningless without the resurrection.

Cycle B

In cycle B, the year of Mark, the gospel readings for the Sundays of Lent are taken from Mark and John. On the first two Sundays we read Mark's account of the tempting of Jesus together with a summary presentation of his mission in Galilee (1:12–15) and his story

18   *Eugene LaVerdiere*

of Jesus' transfiguration (9:2–10). As in cycle A, we then turn to John for the third, fourth and fifth Sundays. Jesus cleanses the temple (Jn 2:13–25), speaks to Nicodemus of eternal life (Jn 3:14–21) and announces the hour of his glorification (Jn 12: 20–33). On these three Sundays, the readings for cycle A (Jn 4:5–42; 9:1–41; 11:1–45) may be substituted, especially at the liturgies which celebrate the scrutinies as part of the *Rite of Christian Initiation of Adults* (RCIA). On Passion Sunday, we normally return to Mark's gospel for the procession with palms (11:1–10), but the alternative is given to read John 12:12–16 in place of Mark. The passion, however, is always from Mark (14:1–15:47). At the Easter Vigil, the gospel reading is Mark's account of the women's visit to the tomb of Jesus (Mk 16:1–8).

The lenten gospel for cycle B thus begins and ends with Mark. His summary of the testing which Jesus experienced after his baptism and of Jesus' missionary preaching, together with his account of the transfiguration, highlight Lent's two-Sunday introduction and announce the season's climax and fulfillment in the supreme test of the passion and the Easter proclamation in the tomb.

FIRST SUNDAY

On the First Sunday of Lent, we join Jesus in the desert for 40 days to prepare for the Christian mission (Mk 1:12–15). He was sent there by the Spirit which had descended on him at baptism and in which he would baptize others (Mk 1:8–9). Jesus' whole life, from the beginning of his ministry to the passion, is presented as a time of testing by Satan. Life's test would be in a wasteland among the wild beasts, but even there God's angels would care for him. It is in that context that Jesus proclaimed the good news of God in Galilee and called everyone to faith and conversion.

Like Jesus, those who heard him would be tested. Would they hear his call to repentance and life, or would they be destroyed by the test? After the waters of the great flood receded, God promised covenant solidarity with human beings and all creation. Never again would he open the floodgates of heaven (Gen 9:8–15). In baptism, we pledge our solidarity with God and find salvation (1 Pt 3:18–22). The entire human race can be saved like Noah and his family at the time of the flood.

SECOND SUNDAY

Last Sunday's gospel showed how Jesus' whole life could be viewed as a test, a preparation for the passion. Today's story of the transfiguration shows how his life was also a preparation for his glorification in the resurrection (Mk 9:2-10). In Mark, the passage comes after a major emphasis on the suffering of those who accepted to be Jesus' followers and model their lives on his (8:31-38). Jesus spoke to them of the passion at some length, but he showed them the resurrection. In their conversation with the risen Lord, the very Law (Moses) and the prophets (Elijah) were transfigured. Peter had declared Jesus the messiah or Christ (8:29). Jesus had spoken of himself as Son of Man (8:31-38). The heavenly voice from the cloud declared Jesus, who was the Christ and the Son of Man, to be God's own beloved Son (9:7). All would become clear once Jesus had risen from the dead (9:9-10).

We are prepared for the transfiguration story by the testing of Abraham (Gen 22:1-2, 9-13, 15-18) and a word of encouragement from Paul's letter to the Romans (8:31-34). God was for Abraham. Who could be against him? Are we finding our own test difficult? Christ Jesus is interceding for us at God's right hand.

THIRD SUNDAY

After the experience of the test and the transfiguration (first and second Sundays) we are ready for the cleansing of the temple (Jn 2:13-25). The scene is very vividly presented. The time is Passover when large crowds are expected in Jerusalem. The place is the temple, transformed into an eastern market. Jesus strikes out. This marketplace was meant to be his Father's house, the home of one whose life and love embrace all. There was no longer any need for Jewish coins, no need for those who changed other currencies into them. There was no need for animal sacrifices. Jesus' sacrifice, his self-offering, the destruction of the temple of his body and its rising in three days, replaced them all and opened the doors of his Father's house to all peoples.

The first reading recalls the attitude and behavior needed to pray and worship in the Father's house (Ex 20:1-17). Christians, like the Israelites before them, profess the commandments as the basis of what God had done for them. We have been brought out of slavery by Christ crucified (1 Cor 1:22-25). For some that may be a stumbling block and for others it may be absurd, but for those who have experienced the freedom of the Father's home, it is power and wisdom.

FOURTH SUNDAY

On the third Sunday, we marveled at the Father's house, a home for all human beings to which all have gained entry by the dying and rising of Christ. Today we return to the same theme, but with an added emphasis. The Father's universal embrace is eternal. The salvation of all who believe is forever (Jn 3:14–21). Jesus' discourse is part of his dialogue with Nicodemus, a prominent Pharisee who came to Jesus during the night. Jesus speaks to Nicodemus, and through him to us, of the reason God sent the Son into the world: that in the Son all who believe might find life eternal. God's Son came as light, and those who are struck by that light find salvation in him. Those who turn away to hide in darkness find condemnation.

The works of darkness and condemnation are illustrated in Chronicles' story of the destruction of the temple and the deportation to Babylon (2 Chr 36:14–17, 19–23). But, as demonstrated in Israel's restoration, God remains merciful, and his loving kindness is forever. We may have been dead in sin, but we are saved in Christ (Eph 2:4–10) as we walk out of darkness into the light.

FIFTH SUNDAY

Again the setting is Jerusalem at Passover time (see Third Sunday) and the crowds have gathered. By now, however, Jesus has become very well known. The word of how Jesus had raised Lazarus from the dead had spread thoughout the land. As the Pharisees saw it, the whole world was running after him. Even the Greeks, Gentiles, wanted to hear him, and it is to them that Jesus announces that the critical hour had come. Jesus speaks with a troubled soul (Jn 12:20–33). (In the synoptic gospels, this was Gethsemane.) Jesus would lay down his life that others might have life, just as a seed dies in the earth to produce an abundance. Those who believe in him must do the same. In giving life they too will find it. In this Jesus would be glorified and his Father would be glorified in him.

The reading from Jeremiah on the interiority of the new covenant whose law would be inscribed not on stone but on the heart

(Jer 31:31–34) prepares us well for Jesus' discourse. So do the reflections in Hebrews (5:7–9). Jesus prayed that he might be saved from death, and God heard his prayer. Through death Jesus found life for himself and for all who know him in faith.

PASSION SUNDAY

The Procession with Palms

The gospel for the procession with palms is Mark 11:1–10, but we also are provided with an alternative reading, John 12:12–16. Both readings present Jesus' solemn entry into Jerusalem.

In Mark, Jesus sends two of his disciples for a colt on which no one has ridden. They follow his precise instructions and return with it. Matthew (cycle A) added mention of an ass to demonstrate how Jesus fulfilled scripture. In Mark emphasis is rather on the fact that no one had yet ridden on the colt. Jesus' entry represented something brand new in Israel. The reign of David which is here celebrated and the real, solemn entry of the Son of David is that of the Son of Man coming in glory at the fulfillment of time (Mk 13:3–37).

John's presentation of the scene is much simpler. There is the crowd to greet Jesus. There are also the shouts of "Hosanna!" However, Jesus himself finds the donkey for his entry. The scriptures would be fulfilled, but the disciples understood none of all this until after Jesus' glorification.

The Liturgy of the Word

The gospel reading is the passion according to Mark (14:1–15:47). For the first and second readings (Is 50:4–7; Phil 2:6–11), see the comments under cycle A.

Mark's passion account is the story of how Jesus died, but it also places great emphasis on how the others in the story were challenged to die with Christ. As Jesus' story, it shows how the enemies of Jesus, who had been conspiring and gathering strength from the beginning of the gospel, finally succeeded in having him put to death. However, it also shows how Jesus' death was not that of a passive victim, but of someone who gave his life for others. As the disciples' story, it shows how those who had accepted Jesus' call to follow him in his life mission struggled to follow through at the time of testing. Solidarity with Christ is not an easy thing. It requires dying with Christ and being buried with Christ. The weaving of the disciples' story into that of Jesus' passion reveals a powerful baptismal undercurrent within Mark's passion narrative.

Cycle C

In cycle C, the year of Luke, all of the gospel readings save one are taken from Luke. For the fifth Sunday, we turn to John. The cycle's basic structure is similar to that of the other two cycles. Lent opens with a two-Sunday introduction, in which Jesus' response to the devil's test (4:1–13) and the transfiguration (9:28–36) prepare us for his victory in the test of his passion (22:14–23:56) and the fulfillment of the transfiguration at Easter (24:1–12). Passion Sunday and Easter Sunday spell out the implications of the victory achieved at the beginning of Jesus' life.

On the third and fourth Sundays we join Luke in exploring the relationship between sin and the evil that befalls us (13:1–9) and the patient, loving mercy with which God deals with us (15:1–3, 11–32). The same emphases, which are part of Luke's pastoral theology of reconciliation, come through in Jesus' dealing with a woman caught in adultery, the fifth Sunday's reading from John (8:1–11). As in cycle B, the readings for the third, fourth and fifth Sundays may be replaced by those of cycle A, especially at the liturgies which celebrate the scrutinies as part of the RCIA.

FIRST SUNDAY

The first Sunday presents Jesus' response to three basic temptations. The first temptation is in the economic sphere. Jesus' response: human needs far exceed the physical. We can hear the echo of Deuteronomy 8:3 in the background: "Not by bread alone . . . , but by every word that comes forth from the mouth of the Lord." The second temptation is political. To gain power over all the kingdoms of the world, Jesus would have to worship the devil. Jesus' response: the price is unacceptable. God alone is to be worshiped. The third temptation is in the religious sphere. Jesus' response: trusting in God must not be distorted into presumption of divine providence.

"My father was a wandering Aramean!" The first reading recalls Israel's positive experience of God the savior and provider. The passage is Deuteronomy 26:4–10, an Israelite profession of faith and gratitude to God who led Israel out of servitude and who sees to people's nourishment. Romans 10:8–13 develops similar themes in a specifically Christian context. The Christian profession of faith leads to salvation.

SECOND SUNDAY

The First Sunday of Lent focused our attention on life's fundamental tests or crises and prepared us for the passion, the ultimate test. The second Sunday dwells on the manifestation of Christ's glory (Lk 9:28b–36). In Luke, the transfiguration takes place while Jesus is at prayer. We recall that a similar manifestation in which Jesus was declared God's beloved Son took place after Jesus' baptism while he was at prayer (3:21–22). Unlike Matthew and Mark, Luke also tells us that the conversation between Jesus, Elijah, and Moses was about Jesus' departure, that is his exodus or ascension, which would take place in Jerusalem. We are thus prepared for Easter and Jesus' return to the Father. In Luke 24:50–53, the ascension takes place on Easter Sunday.

The transfiguration is like the covenant with Abraham (Gn 15:5–12, 17–18), a divine manifestation, but at the same time a promise of future blessing. Just as the promises to Abraham would one day be fulfilled, so also the transfiguration, whose promise was the resurrection and a share in Christ's glory. In Philippians 3:17–4:1, Paul urges the Christians to accept the cross of Christ as a promise of the Lord's coming and of their share in his glory.

THIRD SUNDAY

After the temptations and the transfiguration, we turn to some of life's basic issues for those who join Christ in his response to the test and who have received the promise of resurrection. What are we to think of suffering and death, whether inflicted by others or accidental? Are they the punishment of God for sin and guilt? Jesus' response: In our judgment of others, our answer must be no! In our own case, it may be yes! (Lk 13:1–5) The gospel also includes a parable about an unproductive fig tree growing in a vineyard. The tendency is to want to cut it down. But the vinedresser pleads to be allowed to try at least one more season (Lk 13: 6–9).

With Luke, Christians are to be both kind in their judgments and patient in their efforts.

God does not abandon the people, nor reject them in their affliction. Exodus 3:1-8, the story of the call of Moses at the flaming bush, prepares us to appreciate Jesus' demands in the gospel. God does not reject and destroy, but saves. God is present to the people. Such is his name: "I am who am ever with you" (Ex 3:13-15). All of these events in the Hebrew Scriptures are an example for Christians, to shape their attitude, to warn them, and to help them understand events in their own lives (1 Cor 10:1-6, 10-12).

FOURTH SUNDAY

After reflecting on the basic issue of guilt and retribution, our lenten journey moves on to that of reconciliation. It is not enough to be kind and patient, we must be willing to forgive. Christians, like Jesus, are reconcilers. But how difficult it is to join with others in reconciliation and joyfully to celebrate the return of one who strayed. The gospel shows Pharisees and scribes murmuring when Jesus welcomes sinners and eats with them. Sharing at Jesus' table is a mutual gesture of reconciliation, a proclamation of reconciliation and a celebration of reconciliation (Lk 15:1-3). In the parable, the prodigal son returns home ready to accept the humblest position. The father, overjoyed, celebrates the return of one who had been dead to him. But the older brother refuses to celebrate. Unable to be reconciled, he himself becomes the straying prodigal (Lk 15:11-32).

The theme of forgiveness is introduced in the first reading. As in the gospel, the meal, in this case the Passover, is presented as a celebration of reconciliation. God's promises were being fulfilled (Jos 5:9a, 10-12). Paul focuses on reconciliation as the central ministry of the new covenant. He calls himself and other Christians ambassadors of Christ in the ministry of reconciliation. God has reconciled the world in Christ. And in Christ God continues to do so through Christ's followers (2 Cor 5:17-21).

FIFTH SUNDAY

They led a woman who had been taken in adultery to Jesus and made her stand there before everyone. Our lenten journey takes us into John's gospel (8:1-11). After considering guilt and retribution (third Sunday) and reconciliation (fourth Sunday), we move on to a third basic issue. Those who walk in the light of the passion-resurrection reject hypocrisy, and once reconciled they do not return to their sin. Jesus' words are dramatic: "Let the one who is without sin cast the first stone!" But it is his actions which speak the loudest. Bending down, he writes on the ground with his finger. It is not what he writes that is significant, but that he writes. Ignoring those who would have the woman killed, he doodles. In the silence, they cannot but recognize their own sinfulness and hypocrisy. Alone with the woman, Jesus says simply, "You may go now. Sin no more."

In Isaiah, God says, "Remember not the events of the past. See, I am doing something new" (43:16–21). That is what Jesus was doing in forgiving the sinful woman and rejecting the traditional punishment prescribed by Moses. For Paul, Christ is the only wealth, and justice comes through faith in him. Justification does not come from the observance of the Law (Phil 3:8–14). In our liturgical context, that is also the way the person taken in adultery was justified.

PASSION SUNDAY

The Procession with Palms

As in the other two cycles, today's celebration begins with a special proclamation of the gospel and a procession with palms. We read how Jesus entered Jerusalem and was greeted there not long before the passion, and we re-enact the scene in an entrance procession of our own.

In this year, the gospel is Luke's account of the event (19:28–40). For Luke, Jesus' solemn entry into Jerusalem marks the beginning of the end of his life journey to God, a journey which had begun in Galilee (9:51) and which was to end in heaven at the ascension (24:50–53).

Jesus entered Jerusalem astride an ass on which no one had ridden. Jesus' entry marked something absolutely new. He would come as a king, but like no other. In Matthew and Mark Jesus was greeted as the Son of David. Not so in Luke. Jesus' reign transcended David's reign and every other earthly reign. The people's acclamation echoes the song of the angelic host at Jesus' birth

(2:14), but the entire emphasis is now on heaven: "Peace in heaven and glory in the highest!"

The Liturgy of the Word

In the liturgy of the word, the gospel reading is the passion according to Luke (22:14–23:56). For the first and second readings (Isaiah 50:4–7, Philippians 2:6–11), see the comments under cycle A.

Luke's account of the passion is unique in many ways. For example, the Last Supper (22:14–38), which is like a special prologue for the passion-resurrection account (22:39–24:53), is more elaborate than in the other synoptics. It includes a discourse in which the church's Lord's Supper (22:19–20), the Christian betrayals (22:24–30) and the Christian denials (22:35–38) are held up to the light of the Last Supper (22:14–18), the betrayal which accompanied it (22:21–23) and the denial of Peter (22:31–34).

The interrogation scenes are much more elaborate than in the other gospels. As in Matthew and Mark, we have Jesus before the Sanhedrin (22:63–71) and before Pilate (23:1–6, 13–25), but in Luke we also have him before Herod (23:8–12), whom Jesus a little earlier had called "that fox" (13:31–33). As in his ministry, even in the passion Jesus is the reconciler. This is beautifully presented in the story of the two criminals who were crucified alongside of Jesus (23:32–33, 39–43). "This day you will be with me in paradise" is one of the best remembered lines from Luke's gospel.

EASTERTIME

"Did not the Christ have to suffer all this to enter into his glory?" (Lk 24:26) Without Good Friday and the passion, Easter Sunday and the resurrection would mean very little. Without Lent and a good lenten celebration, the Sundays of Easter would remain empty.

The Easter season presupposes Lent and Lent presupposes Easter. Easter rises on Lent's foundations, and Lent draws its direction, meaning and excitement from Easter. Such is the paschal mystery. In the Easter celebration, which includes the seven Sundays of Easter, the feasts of the Ascension and Pentecost, we celebrate the new life of Christ. The gospel readings, most of which come from John in all three cycles, focus on how that new life of Christ is shared with us and on the demands it makes on us.

Like the other gospels, that according to John has a resurrection narrative (chapter 20 and the gospel's appendix, chapter 21), but in a sense the entire gospel is a resurrection narrative. At Cana, for example, Jesus anticipates his hour, the moment when he would enter into his glory and pour out his Spirit. In the dialogues with Nicodemus and the Samaritan woman, the necessity of being born again and the quenching of thirst are associated with the risen Lord.

The gospel can be read on a first level, that of Jesus, a historical figure, and his disciples, including ourselves. It can also be read on a second level, that of Christ the risen Lord and his followers the Christians. After following Jesus to the passion and resurrection in a first reading, we read the gospel once again in light of the whole experience. When we read a second time, the gospel speaks to us of the life of those who have been baptized, of those who have joined in Jesus' Passover meal and of their life in the company of the risen Lord. In the language of the RCIA, John's gospel is mystagogy.

In all three cycles, the first reading for the seven Sundays of Easter is taken from the Acts of the Apostles, Luke's second volume. We are thus invited to hold up our experience to the struggles and joys of the early Jerusalem community.

The second reading, however, varies from cycle to cycle. In cycle A, we turn to 1 Peter, a letter important for its teaching on the passion-resurrection and its implications for Christian life. In cycle B, the second reading is from 1 John, a letter which seeks to clarify and correct a number of issues which had surfaced in the Johannine community. Its message on love of neighbor is one of the most forceful in the New Testament. Finally in cycle C, our readings come from the book of Revelation, a prophetic book extremely rich in images and steeped in the liturgy of the early church.

Lent is similar to Advent in that both have a well-defined structure. They move systematically along a journey to their climax. Easter like Christmas is a more contemplative season. Struck by the greatness of the event, we approach it over and over again from different angles. Rather than a continuous journey, the readings of Easter describe a continual return to the inexhaustible mystery of the resurrection of Jesus of Nazareth, the one who had been crucified.

Cycle A

EASTER SUNDAY

Year after year the entire church gathers early in the morning of the first day of the week at the tomb of Jesus. It is Easter, and we celebrate the new creation. The tomb, which normally would be a symbol of death, an ending, becomes a symbol of life, a beginning. In Jesus, the old Adam died; in the risen Lord, the new Adam bursts into life.

The gospel reading for all three cycles is John 20:1-9. (However, an alternative reading is also provided for each cycle. In cycle A that reading is Matthew's account (28:1-10) of the women's visit to the tomb.) In John's account, the empty tomb is, at first, bad news. Accompanying Mary Magdalene, we find the tomb open and run off to Simon Peter and the disciple whom Jesus loved with the news that "the Lord has been taken from the tomb" (Jn 20:1-2). It is still dark. Jesus was the light who had come into a world of darkness. For the time being that darkness still enveloped us, but it would not overcome the light (Jn 1:5).

We then join Peter and the other disciple for a second visit to the tomb. This time the darkness would be dispelled and the empty tomb would become good news. With the beloved disciple, we respectfully defer to Peter, the rock of our Christian tradition. The burial wrappings had expressed Jesus' identity in death; they have been left behind. Jesus is risen. The shroud cannot be his garment (Jn 20:4-10).

The alternative reading from Matthew, which is read at the Easter Vigil, is quite different. The event is transformed into a theophany. Mary has gone to the tomb with a companion. There is an earthquake. The angel of the Lord descends and rolls back the stone. At his dazzling appearance the guards stationed there are paralyzed with fear. The women, however, are given a mission to bring the good news of the resurrection to Jesus' disciples. On their way, the Lord Jesus himself appears to them and sends them with his peace to his brothers. They would see him in Galilee (Mt 28:1-10). Like John, Matthew grasps for images to express the inexpressible.

The first reading is the same for all three cycles (Acts 10:34, 37-43). Peter is in a Gentile household, that of Cornelius, an important military personage. Recognizing the presence of the Spirit, he proclaims the gospel of Jesus' life, death and resurrection to the Gentiles. His commission to preach comes from sharing at the Lord's table. United to the Lord of all (10:36), Peter and the church have no choice but to reach out to all.

Like the first reading, the second is read in all three cycles. We are raised up in company with Christ. Our new life in glory will be manifest when Christ's life is fully revealed (Col 3:1-4). For the second reading, we are also given an alternative, which like the main reading is the same for all three cycles. Yeast is a corrupting agent. We must rid ourselves of the old yeast in our lives. We must become an unleavened bread of sincerity and truth (1 Cor 5:6b-8).

For evening Masses on Easter Sunday the church recommends that the story of the disciples of Emmaus be read as the gospel (Lk 24:13-35). This too, is for all the cycles. This beautiful story is everyone's favorite. We identify easily with the two discouraged disciples. They had been given what appeared to be good news, but it had become bad news. They had been hopeful, but their hopes had collapsed in the crucifixion of Jesus. There were reports that he was alive, but where was he? All the while, the disciples were speaking to Jesus himself. Upon welcoming one who seemed but a stranger to them and joining him in a meal, their eyes were opened in recognition and with hearts burning they hastened to bring the good news to the others.

Hopes fulfilled beyond all expectations, hospitality, burning hearts, eagerness to share our faith, that is what Easter is all about.

SECOND SUNDAY OF EASTER

Our gospel reading is the original ending of John's gospel (20:19-31). We join the disciples behind locked doors in fear. What had been done to Jesus could be done to us, but the Lord Jesus does not abandon us. He joins us in the prison we have built around ourselves, gives us his peace, and as one who has known persecution—witness his wounds—he sends us as he was sent. He did not hide, neither must we. Gifted with his Spirit, we are sent to be reconcilers. With Thomas we face the wounds of Jesus and with him we believe, even though we have not seen Jesus with our physical eyes. For John, this is the end of the story of Jesus' signs. In reading it, may we all be strengthened in faith and may we have life in his name.

A summary of life in the early Jerusalem community is our first reading (Acts 2:42–47). Luke's idealized presentation of sharing in the church's golden age holds up a vision for every age. Teaching like the apostles taught, united in spirit, joining in the breaking of bread, and open in prayer, such is our vision. In the second reading, we sing of our new life. We have been reborn through our baptismal association with the risen Lord. Our hope should sustain us in difficult times, but we need to be purified, as even gold has to be purified. Reborn, we must then grow up (1 Pt 1:3–9).

THIRD SUNDAY OF EASTER

For the gospel reading (Lk 24:13–35), see Easter Sunday and the gospel suggested for evening Masses.

In the first reading, we join Peter, the Eleven and a large crowd of Jews living in Jerusalem. It is Pentecost, and Peter rises for his first great discourse. The section of the discourse which forms our reading (Acts 2:14, 22–28) dwells on the extraordinary life of Jesus, his crucifixion, his resurrection and the witness of the scriptures. The passage Peter quotes is Psalm 16:8–11, in which the psalmist proclaims his trust that God never will abandon him to corruption. With 1 Peter 1:17–21, we recognize that our liberation from a futile way of life was purchased by the blood of Christ, whom God has raised from the dead.

FOURTH SUNDAY OF EASTER

A sheepfold, a gate, a shepherd, sheep and thieves or strangers, such are the images of today's gospel (Jn 10:1–10). The passage is from one of Jesus' discourses. In a first development, Jesus addresses the difference between true and false shepherds. The true shepherd is one who enters the sheepfold through the gate. The sheep recognize him when he calls them by name and they follow him out. Not so the stranger, whom the sheep flee and whose voice they do not recognize. Recall how in John 20:16, Mary Magdalene recognizes the Lord's voice when he calls her by name. In a second development, Jesus explains that he is the gate of the sheepfold. A true shepherd and the sheep enter the sheepfold through him. As the gate he stands between the sheep and false shepherds who would steal, slaughter and destroy the sheep.

As on the third Sunday, the first reading is from Peter's great Pentecost discourse, a summary of Christian preaching, just as Acts 2:42–47 is a summary of Christian living (see second Sunday). The passage describes the enthusiastic response to Peter's proclamation of the gospel (Acts 2:14a, 36–41). In 1 Peter 2:20b–25, we have a link between Peter's discourse in Acts and John 10. At one time we were straying like sheep, but now we have returned to the sheepfold.

FIFTH SUNDAY OF EASTER

This Sunday and on the following two Sundays, the gospel reading is from Jesus' great discourse at the Last Supper (Jn 14–17). Jesus is soon to go away but the disciples must not be troubled, for the purpose of his departure is to prepare a place for them in his Father's house. Afterwards he will return to them and bring them with him (14:1–4). In today's reading (14:1–12), Jesus' discourse is twice interrupted, first by Thomas who asks about the way to where Jesus is going (14:5) and then by Philip who requests that Jesus show them the Father (14:8). The two questions occasion two short developments, one on Jesus himself as the way to the Father (14:6–7), the other on Jesus as the manifestation of the Father who dwells in him (14:9–12).

Acts 6:1–7 introduces a new part of Acts (6:1–12:25), which climaxes in the establishment of the church at Antioch. As we often find today, the disciples are overwhelmed by the demands of the ministry and have no time for prayer and the ministry of the word. For their part, the poor are not being well-served. The community, together with the apostles, responds by diversifying the ministries and drawing new people to serve from sources that had not yet been tapped. With 1 Peter 2:4–9 we celebrate the church, whose members have been reborn. It is a stone edifice with Jesus as its cornerstone. For disbelievers the stone is an obstruction, but for believers it is of great value: they are a chosen race, a people claimed as God's own.

SIXTH SUNDAY OF EASTER

Today's gospel reading (Jn 14:15-21) is from the continuation of Jesus' response to Philip (see fifth Sunday). In his earthly life Jesus has been a paraclete, a teacher and intercessor, for his followers. He is about to leave them, but he will ask his Father to send them another paraclete, the Spirit of truth, during his absence. One day he will return and reveal his love to them. Both gifts, that of the paraclete and that of Jesus' love, are contingent on their having loved him and kept his commandments.

The second reading (1 Pt 3:15-18) prepares us for the gospel. Christians are to venerate the Lord who dwells in their hearts. They are to remain calm, gentle and respectful even when persecuted. They must even be a people of hope. After all, Christ died for their sins to lead them to God. Acts 8:5-8, 14-17 describes the marvelous reception the Samaritans gave Philip and his gospel message as well as the subsequent work of Peter and John among them.

ASCENSION

The commission of the apostles marks the conclusion of Matthew's gospel (Mt 28:16-20). The setting is a mountain in Galilee, where Jesus the risen Lord appears to the eleven. Judas, whose death was described in Mt 27:3-10 has not been replaced. Until now some of the eleven may have doubted about the resurrection, but no more. Their mission is to be universal. They are to baptize all nations and teach them to live as Jesus had taught them to live. In all this they could count on his presence and solidarity with them to the end.

The first reading, taken from the introduction of the Acts of the Apostles, also deals with the universal mission of the church (Acts 1:1-11). It opens with a brief preface recapitulating the gospel, Luke's first volume, but then, seemingly midstream, the author "disappears" and he allows Jesus the risen Lord to take over. The universal mission, which summarizes Acts, rests on the authority of the risen Lord. After the commission, Jesus ascends to the Father, leaving the apostolic community to form the church and pursue its mission.

In Ephesians 1:17-23 Paul invokes a blessing on the Ephesian community and celebrates the power of God in those who believe, a power already revealed in the resurrection of Jesus and his ascension to God's right hand.

SEVENTH SUNDAY OF EASTER

John 17, the longest of the prayers attributed to Jesus in the New Testament, forms the conclusion of his discourse at the Last Supper. Today we read from the first part of the discourse, in which Jesus speaks to his Father of the work which he has accomplished (17:1-8). His hour has come. He has glorified his Father; he has prepared his disciples to continue the work which had been entrusted to him. Let his Father now glorify him. We also read from the beginning of the prayer's second section where Jesus prays for his disciples (17:9-11a). Our first reading is the conclusion of the special prologue for the Acts of the Apostles (1:12-14). Immediately after the ascension (see notes for Ascension), the apostles returned to Jerusalem from the Mount of Olives and devoted themselves to prayer with Mary the mother of Jesus and his brothers. This last statement (1:14) is an important little summary for showing how the early church viewed the position of Mary in the apostolic community. With 1 Peter we reflect on how we ought to rejoice if we are called to suffer for being Christians (1 Pt 4:13-16).

VIGIL OF PENTECOST

We are approaching the end of our Easter journey. It is the eve of Pentecost. The gospel reading announces the coming of the Spirit (Jn 7:37-39). Jesus invites all who thirst and who believe in him to come to him and quench their thirst. With a text inspired by Isaiah 12:3 or perhaps by Moses' tapping of the rock in the exodus, Jesus recalls his discussion with the Samaritan woman at the well and announces the outflowing of the water, the Spirit, from his side at his death on the cross: "From within him rivers of living water shall flow" (7:38).

The story of the tower of Babel (Gen 11:1-9), with the origin of the human race's inability to communicate and the confusion of tongues, forms the first reading. The story presents the last in a series of original sins, which wants to usurp God's position in the heavens. Pentecost, when the apostles would speak in their own language but in such a way that all would hear them in their own, responds to this "original sin." We also have three alternative readings, one from Exodus with the great theophany at Sinai (19:3–8a, 16–20b), one from Ezekiel, the vision of the dry bones and their resurrection through the power of the Spirit (37:1–14), and one from Joel, with its description of the future outpouring of the Spirit (3:1–5). The second reading presents the Spirit as the first fruits of the world's redemption. That same Spirit assists us in our weakness and intercedes for us before God (Rom 8:22–27).

PENTECOST

For the gospel, see the Second Sunday of Easter. John 20:19–23, in which the risen Lord breathes the Spirit into his disciples, evokes the figure of God breathing life into Adam's inert clay and making him a living being. What Luke situated on the Jewish Feast of Pentecost, John situated on Easter.

The opening reading is Luke's account of the Pentecost event (Acts 2:1–11). The sound like a strong, driving wind recalls the first creation account in Genesis when a mighty wind swept over the primeval waters. The tongues, which are like fire, announce the apostolic ministry which is finally to cast fire on the earth (see Lk 12:49). The scene describes a gathering of the Jews from every nation. Throughout the then known world they would be the gateway to the Gentile mission. They spoke a babel of tongues, but each one was able to turn to another and say, "These apostles are speaking my language!" Pentecost was reversing the disarray of Babel (see Vigil of Pentecost).

As the second reading we have part of an important teaching of Paul on spiritual gifts (1 Cor 12:3b–7, 12–13): "No one can say: 'Jesus is Lord,' except through the Holy Spirit." After that resounding introduction, Paul stresses the unity of the gifts by reason of their coming from the same Spirit. Our origins and backgrounds are insignificant. Are we not all members of one body, all of us who have been baptized into one body and who have been given to drink of the one Spirit?

Cycle B

EASTER SUNDAY

All the readings but one are the same as in cycle A (Acts 10:34, 37-43; Col 3:1-4 or 1 Cor 5:6b-8; Jn 20:1-9 or in the evening Lk 24:13-35). The one exception is Mark 16:1-8, which is suggested as an alternative for the gospel at morning and daytime celebrations. Mark's account of the women's visit to the tomb is also read at the Easter Vigil in the B cycle.

The women are concerned about the stone which sealed the entrance to the tomb of Jesus. Who will roll it back for them? That stone blocked the way to life. It was a huge stone. Contrary to the women's expectations, no human being could possibly roll away that stone. God alone could and did. A young man in the tomb proclaims life to them in the midst of all the signs of death. Jesus is risen! The young man proclaiming the gospel is dressed in the garments of the risen Lord. As Christians shall we run away with our lips locked in fear or shall we join the young man in sharing the gospel?

SECOND SUNDAY OF EASTER

For the gospel reading (Jn 20:19-31), see the Second Sunday of Easter, cycle A.

As in cycle A (Acts 2:42-47), the liturgy of the word opens with a summary of the life of the primitive Christian community at Jerusalem (Acts 4:32-35). The first summary, however, was more general. This time we focus on one aspect of the community's life, the sharing of goods in common, and on the power with which those Christians witnessed to the resurrection. It is not that no one retained possessions. Rather, each thought of what he or she owned as belonging to all. The needs of the others limited a Christian's right to property. With 1 John 5:1-6, we then reflect on how those who are begotten of God love the Father and every child he has begotten.

THIRD SUNDAY OF EASTER

We begin with the conclusion of the story of Emmaus (Lk 24:35; see the suggested reading for Masses in the evening of Easter Sunday, cycle A). The two disciples have rejoined the community assembled in Jerusalem. While they are still speaking of their experience, Jesus himself stands in their midst. The story corrects the mistaken impression of some: relating to Christ is a matter of flesh, bones and hunger, not just a matter of spirit. In the risen Lord, suffering and hungry humanity reaches out to the church (24:36–45). As such, the Lord's appearance provides the basis for the church's universal mission (24:46–48).

The first reading (Acts 3:13–15, 17–19) is from Peter's second discourse. As on Pentecost (see cycle A, third and fourth Sundays of Easter), Peter summarizes the gospel message for the crowd. Its message to Peter's "fellow Israelites" is now addressed to all of us. Its focus on Peter's original addressees, when there were as yet no Gentiles in the church, is understandable. Today, however, it speaks to us all as Peter spoke to the Jews. It is through us human beings that Jesus came to his death. Jesus Christ is an offering not for our sins alone but for the whole world. When we keep his commandments, God's very own love becomes perfect in us (1 Jn 2:1–5a).

FOURTH SUNDAY OF EASTER

As on the fourth Sunday of cycle A, we read part of Jesus' "good shepherd" discourse (Jn 10:11–18). In cycle A, we saw how Jesus is the gate of the sheepfold (10:1–10). In cycle B, we reflect on him as the good shepherd. Jesus gives his life for his sheep. At the gate he stood ready to lay down his life were anyone to try to harm the sheep. In today's reading, this emphasis is made even more explicit. Further, Jesus is not shepherd to those alone who already are part of his flock but to all the others as well. The vision of John 10 is that there be but one flock, as there is but one true shepherd, the good shepherd.

Peter's third discourse in Jerusalem is our first reading (see third Sunday, cycle B; the third and fourth Sundays, cycle A). In the first discourse, Peter had addressed the crowds who milled around the apostles in the city. In the second, he spoke to those who had gathered in the temple at the hour of prayer. On this third occasion, he speaks to the Sanhedrin, Jerusalem's religious governing body (Acts 4:8–12). With 1 John 3:1–2, we celebrate God's love which made us his children and which reminds us that if the world did not recognize God's Son, we hardly can expect it to recognize us.

FIFTH SUNDAY OF EASTER

This Sunday and on the following two Sundays the gospel reading is taken from Jesus' farewell discourse at the Last Supper (Jn 14–17). Jesus is the true vine, and the Father is the vinedresser (15:1). The image of the vine is developed in two stages. First, Jesus speaks of the pruning of the vine's branches to increase their yield. Then he identifies the branches as his followers. Those who live in him produce an abundant yield. Those who don't live in him wither and die, and they must be pruned away (15:2–8).

The first reading is from Acts. It treats of Paul's dramatic escape from Damascus, of how he was introduced to the community at Jerusalem by Barnabas, and of his evangelization work in Jerusalem (9:26–31). The persecution which followed gives us a taste of what was to come as the persecutor more and more becomes the persecuted. The second reading (1 Jn 3:18–24) speaks of our need as God's children to love one another in action and in truth, not merely in words. Only so do we remain in God's love.

SIXTH SUNDAY OF EASTER

The gospel reading sums up the entire ethic of Jesus. His disciples are to love one another. Only in this way will their lives be fruitful. The foundations of this ethic lie in God's own love. The Father has loved Jesus, and Jesus has loved his disciples in the same way. Thus it is that the Father's love, incarnate in that Jesus, reaches out to the disciples. The disciples who live and dwell in the love of Jesus are thus able to love one another. Jesus' love flows through their lives and reaches out to others (Jn 15:9–17).

The first reading is from the book of Acts (10:25–26, 34–35, 44–48). For comment on a portion of this passage, see Easter Sunday, cycle A. This Sunday's reading includes the encounter between Peter and Cornelius (10:25–26), a portion of Peter's discourse (10:34–35), and the baptism of Cornelius' entire household (10:44–48). The second reading (1 Jn 4:7–10) develops the theme of love among those who were begotten of God and sets the stage for a similar development in the gospel.

ASCENSION

The original ending of Mark's gospel was at 16:8. The canonical text of the gospel, however, includes an additional ending (16:9-20). Our reading for Ascension Thursday is taken from this passage. It summarizes the ending of Luke's gospel and adds a number of signs which will accompany those who proclaim the good news to all of creation. Such signs, especially the handling of serpents and the drinking of poison are not to be taken literally. They evoke poetry such as we find in Isaiah and are associated with the idyllic age which is to follow the fulfillment of history.

For the first and second readings (Acts 1:1-12, Eph 1:17-23), see cycle A.

SEVENTH SUNDAY OF EASTER

The gospel reading is taken from the prayer of Jesus which concludes his discourse at the Last Supper (Jn 17:11b-19). For the first part of this prayer, see seventh Sunday, cycle A. In today's segment, Jesus' concern is with his disciples. While he was with them, he had protected them. Now that he was to leave them, he asks that his Father guard them, especially in times of persecution.

The first reading is from Acts (1:15-17, 20a, 20c-26). In it we join the early community in Jerusalem for the selection of an apostle to replace Judas. The man would be Matthias. With the apostolic Twelve now complete again, Luke's second volume is ready to take up the story of the church in Jerusalem. The second reading is 1 John 4: 11-16. Its message on Christian love concludes with the remarkable statement that God is love, and one who abides in love abides in God, and God abides in that person.

VIGIL OF PENTECOST AND PENTECOST

See the notes for cycle A.

Cycle C

EASTER SUNDAY

All the readings but one are the same as in cycle A (Acts 10:34, 37-43; Col 3:1-4 or 1 Cor 5:6b-8; Jn 20:1-9 or in the evening

Lk 24:13–35). The one exception is Luke 24:1–12, which is suggested as an alternative for the gospel at morning and daytime celebrations. Luke's account of the women's visit to the tomb is also read at the Easter Vigil in the C cycle.

Luke's retelling of the women's visit to the tomb is very different from the others. In Matthew, they encounter an angel at the tomb. In Mark, they find a young man inside the tomb. In Luke, there are two men, prophetic teachers, elders, who ask why the women seek one who is living in a place for the dead. They should seek him among the living. The elders also interpret the event of the passion in light of Jesus' teaching. What had been a prediction of the passion now becomes a flashback. Finally they commission the women to bring the news to the others, and this the women do. Upon hearing the news, Peter goes to the tomb personally. Every Easter morning, we join him in his amazement.

SECOND SUNDAY OF EASTER

For the gospel reading (Jn 20:19–31), see the notes for the Second Sunday of Easter, cycle A.

As in cycles A (Acts 2:42–47) and B (Acts 4:32–35), our readings open with one of Luke's summaries of life in the primitive Christian community at Jerusalem (Acts 5:12–16). This is the third and final such summary. It focuses on the signs and wonders which occurred through the hands of the apostles and on the large numbers which were continually added to the Lord. Those who share like the early community become a healing presence in their own communities. The second reading is taken from the vision of John at the beginning of the Book of Revelation (1:9–11a, 12–13, 17–19). The description of Christ in glory evokes the great prophetic visions of the Old Testament, notably those of Ezekiel 1:1–3:15 and Daniel 7.

THIRD SUNDAY OF EASTER

An extraordinary catch of fish, a meal with the Lord on the seashore, and the mission of Peter, these are the elements of today's reading (Jn 21:1–19), which includes most of the appendix of John's gospel. Seven of the disciples follow Peter's lead and go out fishing. All night they fish but catch nothing, until at the suggestion of Jesus whom they do not yet recognize, they cast their nets on the other side and make an extraordinary catch. The catch is symbolic of the future response to the Christian mission. Once they had recognized Jesus and joined him on the shore, they accepted his invitation to share his meal, a sign of solidarity with him. The meal provides the grounds for the mission which is then given to Peter. Jesus' triple question, "Do you love me?" calls to mind Simon's triple denial (18:15–18, 25–27).

In the first reading (Acts 5:27b–32, 40b–41) we have the second time that Peter and the apostles appeared before the Sanhedrin (see notes for the fourth Sunday, cycle B). The passage includes the High Priest's interrogation and Peter's response as well as the trial's outcome. Peter's response echoes his other discourses in Acts. The second reading is from the vision of the scroll and the Lamb in the Book of Revelation (5:11–14). Its description of a heavenly liturgy includes two short hymns honoring Christ the Lamb.

FOURTH SUNDAY OF EASTER

As in cycles A and B, the theme for the Fourth Sunday of Easter is again Jesus the good shepherd. In cycle A, we read John 10:1–10, and in B we read John 10:11–18. Today, our reading is John 10:27–30, part of Jesus' response to the request, "If you really are the Messiah, tell us in plain words" (10:24). Those who are Jesus' sheep know the answer. They hear his voice and follow him, and he gives them eternal life, something no one can take away from them. They are in the hand of Jesus, and that means they are in the Father's hand as well.

Paul's preaching in the synagogue at Antioch in Pisidia (Acts 13:16–41) is patterned on the discourses of Peter in Acts. Our reading includes part of its introduction (13:14) and its sequel (13:43–52). Invited to speak again on the following sabbath, a huge crowd of Gentiles also came to hear him, and this proved a source of dissension. It is at this point that Paul turned to the Gentiles with the message of salvation. A persecution followed, and Paul and Barnabas had to leave town. The second reading (Rev 7:9, 14b–17) celebrates the triumph of the elect. Like the reading for the third Sunday, it includes an early Christian hymn.

FIFTH SUNDAY OF EASTER

The scene for the gospel is the Last Supper. Judas has just left, and Jesus gives a brief discourse (Jn 13:31–33a, 34–35). The time has come for his glorification and departure, and so he gives his disciples a new commandment of love. The disciples are to love one another in the same way that Jesus has loved them. This will be a sign that they are his disciples. The discourse provides the immediate setting for Jesus' exchange with Peter about his future denial (13:36–38) and sets out some of the basic themes of his farewell discourse (chap. 14–17).

The return of Paul and Barnabas to Antioch at the end of the missionary journey is more than a brief travelogue. As they left each place, the two missionaries spoke of the trials which the communities could expect, and they installed presbyters in each church. The first reading (Acts 14:21–27) thus indicates the origins of the church structure which continued to the time of the writing of Acts. The reading from Revelation (21:1–5a) is from the introduction to the book's description of the new creation, in which God will dwell among us and we shall be his people. The description (21:1–22:5) was inspired in part by Isaiah 65:17–25 but especially by Ezekiel 40–48.

SIXTH SUNDAY OF EASTER

Today's gospel is taken from Jesus' last discourse in John's gospel (Jn 14:23–29). In it Jesus distinguishes between what he had taught his disciples and what the paraclete, that is the Holy Spirit, would do for them. Jesus' teaching had focused on love, being true to his word, the Father's love for one who was true, the way the Lord Jesus and the Father would dwell in him or her, and the sending of the paraclete. The paraclete would both instruct them in everything as they made their way through history and would remind them of what Jesus had taught. After this brief statement (14:23–26), Jesus announces that his farewell to them is "peace," and he asks that they rejoice with him at his return to his Father.

The first reading is taken from Acts. It includes the introduction to the great assembly at Jerusalem (15:1–2) and the decisions of this assembly, or council, as it is sometimes called (15:22–29). The Gentiles would not have to become Jewish or be subject to the Law in order to be Christians. The second reading (Rev 21:10–14,

22–23) continues the description of the new creation and the new Jerusalem (see notes for the fifth Sunday).

ASCENSION

The church's universal mission and the story of the ascension as told in Luke 24:46–53 forms the gospel for today. Note the way Jesus blesses the assembly as he ascends. The promises made to Abraham that in his progeny all peoples would be blessed were being fulfilled. The ascension scene is thus intimately related to the universal mission statement which preceded it. Note also that the community returns to the temple and praises God after Jesus has returned to his Father. What Jesus does in the Father's heavenly dwelling, they do in his earthly dwelling. For the first and second readings (Acts 1:1–11; Eph 1:17–23) see cycle A.

SEVENTH SUNDAY OF EASTER

As on the seventh Sunday of cycles A and B, we draw our gospel reading from the prayer which acts as the conclusion of Jesus' farewell discourse (Jn 17:20–26). In this portion of the prayer, Jesus prays for all who, through the words of his followers, will come to believe in him. They too must be one with him, with the Father and with his present followers. Jesus had revealed the Father's name to his disciples. He would continue to reveal it to all those who would come to him in the future. To appreciate Jesus' prayer, it is necessary to identify with him and to join him in prayer as he addresses the Father directly.

The first reading (Acts 7:55–60) tells of the death of Stephen, his vision of the Son of Man and his prayer that his executioners be forgiven, a prayer which recalls Jesus' own prayer as he was dying on the cross. It also introduces Saul, who would soon be playing a major role in the Christian mission. The second reading (Rev 22:12–14, 16–17, 20) is from the conclusion of the Book of Revelation. It multiplies the titles of Jesus and the yearnings of Christians for his coming.

VIGIL OF PENTECOST AND PENTECOST

See the notes for cycle A.

The Lectionary
for Easter

Cheryl E. Dieter
Brian L. Helge

From the Great Vigil of Easter through the celebration of the festival of Pentecost, the church's liturgy is single-minded in its preoccupation with the resurrection of the Lord Jesus Christ. For 50 days—a week of weeks, an octave of octaves—we are immersed in celebration of this glorious "day which the Lord has made," and the vast significance of this day's event for the life of the Christian community and the baptized people who constitute that community. What the church so joyously celebrates in the most holy night of the Lord's Pasch, the lectionary of the Great Fifty Days seeks to explicate. In fact, no season of the church's observance shows greater coherence in pericope selections than Easter. The meaning of the eight Sunday Masses of the Easter season is not embedded in any internal logic of these Masses, but in the liturgical structure of the Vigil that begins the sequence.

The coherences of the Masses of the Easter season center in the church's understanding of the connections between resurrection and new life, the empty tomb, the post-resurrection appearances of the Lord, Sunday, baptism, (and confirmation-chrismation), the holy eucharist, and the assembly that celebrates this constellation of events and concepts. Once this foundational complex of events and images (first brought together in the liturgy of the Vigil) is firmly established as the interpretive principle, the overarching coherence of the pericopes for Easter emerges almost effortlessly.

But the coherence of the Masses for the eight Sundays of Easter is not developed thematically. It stems from the unitary vision of the church as it gazes upon the resurrection of Jesus. Jesus is risen from the dead and the implications of this astounding declaration are many and staggering.

Some futher note needs to be made, however, about the interior "thematic unity" of the pericopes appointed for any single Mass. If the selections for a given Mass are dealt with in isolation from the overarching coherence of the seasonal series and outside the context of the central organizing significance of the Vigil, no connections are apparent. Any approach is too wooden that seeks to impose a thematic connection on all three pericopes for a given Mass of the eight-Sunday series. Such an approach will fail—or it will find a "theme" that is simply not there. It is well worth the effort to seek the meaning of each Mass's pericopes within the larger liturgical and seasonal context, but the desire to harmonize the rich textures of the pericopes into a single, handy, homogenized word or phrase is a temptation that must be resisted.

New Vision, New Life

Another perspective on these pericopes that requires note is the coherence we gain for them by reading them in their biblical context. Thus, in reflecting on the pericopes in the book of Acts assigned to the Masses of Easter, we must remember that these narratives relate events in the life of the church as it first came to terms with the reality of the resurrection of Jesus and with the reality of the content of the apostolic faith embodied in its kerygmatic preaching. Having celebrated all that Jesus began to do and to teach, we now fix our gaze on all that Jesus continues to do and teach in this church since his resurrection.

The First Letter of Peter (year A) is thought by many scholars to have been a homily on resurrection or baptism, perhaps even an exposition of an ancient baptismal hymn or creed. The First Letter of John (year B) describes the kind of people we are free to be in light of the resurrection of Jesus and our participation in that event of liberation through baptism. Sin, death and the evil one have been vanquished; we can live in love. And, having entered this "end of all the ages" initiated in Jesus' death and resurrection, we are given, in the

Book of Revelation (year C), potent images of the consummation of this event, a vision of the universe in which all the zigzag and circuitous routes of history and our personal lives find their *telos* (end and meaning) at the feet of the risen and glorified Jesus.

The reading from the gospel of John likewise provides a unity of theological perspective; and several of the non-Johannine gospel pericopes clearly have parallel motifs in the fourth gospel (e.g., Luke 24:13-35; John 21:1ff). The appearance narratives and the material drawn from the Farewell Discourse manifest remarkable similarities when read in the context of the Easter event and its explication during these weeks after the Vigil.

Several pericopes are of crucial significance to the entire series of selections for this season and may even be viewed as the "controlling lessons" for the continuing explication of the significance of the Vigil's proclamation during the eight Sundays of Easter. The gospel pericope is not among these; it follows in the series of readings that begins on Palm Sunday (which has been in place at least since the fourth century in Jerusalem). These gospels recount the historical events, from Jesus' entry into Jerusalem through the resurrection, on the appropriate days. In this historicized series of pericopes, Easter Day, the First Sunday of Easter, is devoted to the empty tomb.

Christians Assembled, the Body of Christ

The pericope from John 20:19-31 (the gospel for the Second Sunday of Easter in all three years) brings together several crucial threads to inform the selection of lessons for the season of Easter. The assembly of the disciples takes place on the day of the Lord's resurrection, the first day of the week, Sunday; and again "eight days later," i.e., again on the first day of the week, Sunday. And the Lord himself comes to these weekly assemblies of the disciples. He himself is in the midst of them and is recognized by them. Thomas, absent the first time the disciples assembled, sees and recognizes the Lord and comes to faith only in the context of this Sunday assembly of the faithful; he does not come alone and he does not come to faith, despite the witness of the other disciples, apart from the Sunday assembly.

It is instructive to note that the first part of the pericope, John 20:19–23 (Pentecost ABC), recurs as the selection for the Mass on the last day of the Great Fifty Days, thus indicating the inseparable connection between the Easter event and the gift of the Holy Spirit in the church. In view of the baptismal imagery of the Vigil it becomes the task of the church during the whole of the Easter season to explicate its own nature—to explain the life of the assembly as constituted by baptized believers who have received the gifts of the Holy Spirit and who gather in weekly assembly to recall the resurrection of the Lord Jesus. The life of the baptized is not only the individuals' initiation into the death and resurrection of Jesus. It is also the life of the body of Christ.

The gospel pericopes appointed for the Third Sunday of Easter are, likewise, crucial selections drawn together from the several strands of thought upon which the church concentrates during this time. The narrative of the walk to Emmaus (Luke 24:13–48) is appointed for years A and B (to verse 35 for year A and from verse 35 to the end for year B). Again, the events recounted take place on the day of the Lord's resurrection, the first day of the week, Sunday, and in the second part of the pericope, the part appointed for year B, the disciples are gathered together. The two disciples on the road do not recognize the Lord, even though their conversation is about his death and resurrection and about the central writings of the covenant, the Law and the prophets. Indeed, they only recognize their participation in this post-resurrection event when Jesus does with them what the assembly of believers does at its gatherings. As he had done at the Last Supper, Jesus takes bread, blesses it, breaks it, and gives it to them. The recurrence of formula from the eucharistic institution narrative, here and in all the feeding-of-the-multitude narratives, is surely intentional. Read in the liturgical context of this series of Easter pericopes, these narratives are yet another indication of the nature and quality of life in the community of those who have been baptized and now share in the resurrected life of the body of Christ. Similar motifs of bread sharing in the context of a gathering of disciples are provided in the narrative of Jesus' appearance on the beach of the Sea of Tiberias (John 21:1–19), the appointed reading for the Third Sunday of Easter (year C). Again, there is a gathering of disciples; Jesus appears;

unrecognition gives way to recognition—"It is the Lord"(and no one says that Jesus is Lord except by the Spirit); they share the bread.

The pericope of Peter's preaching on the occasion of Cornelius' baptism (Acts 10:34–43), itself a primitive kerygma, is appointed to be read in all three years on the First Sunday of Easter. The paragraph preceding this text recounts Cornelius' vision of a man in bright apparel (a vision, perhaps of the resurrected Lord himself). The passage immediately following describes the gift of the Spirit as well as the baptism of Cornelius and his household and friends. This also takes place in the context of an assembly of the faithful; when Peter goes to Caesarea, "some of the brethren from Joppa accompanied him" (Acts 10:23).

The Petrine preaching itself encapsulates the content of the earliest witness to the resurrection of Jesus and its significance. Within this framework and in light of the overarching coherences we have been tracing throughout the liturgical contexts, we are confronted with a startlingly explicit proclamation of the eucharistic nature of this resurrection faith and life. "God raised him on the third day and made him manifest; not to all the people but to us who were chosen by God, who ate and drank with him after he rose from the dead" (vs. 40–41). This entire pericope, standing as the first reading at the first Mass after the celebration of the Great Vigil, is the epitome of the Vigil's meaning and the text that sets the thematic structure for the entire season to come. It is unfortunate that the context of the proclamation has been omitted by the designers of the lectionary; an even stronger thematic comment would have resulted had the pericope included Peter's company and the gift of the Spirit and the baptisms.

Believers' Baptism, the Gifts of the Spirit

Once these lectionary selections and their controlling importance have been perceived, it is short work to find these same critical thematic threads throughout the series of pericopes for the eight Sundays of Easter. We have already noted the tremendous importance attached to the weekly gathering of the assembly of believers on the first day of the week. To those pericopes already mentioned, we may add the use of Acts 2:1–11 (Pentecost A,B,C) which also points most likely to a Sunday event. Surely this was another of those first days of the week so significant for the gift of the Spirit and baptisms, and for the proclamation of the death and resurrection of Jesus.

The daily life of the community of the baptized is also described in the book of Acts. Of particular note are Acts 2:42–47 for Easter 2A and Acts 4:32–35 for Easter 2B. In the first of these (Acts 2:42ff), the community's life and daily prayer are described; in the second (Acts 4:32ff), its testimony to the resurrection and its unity. Acts 2:1–11 (Pentecost A,B,C) indicates the universality of the gospel of the resurrection ("from all nations") and the constituting role of the Holy Spirit.

Even the "practical" aspects of the life of the community happen within the context of the resurrection of Jesus and the accompanying gift of the Spirit. Thus, Acts 6:1–7 (Easter 5A) recounts the election of the first deacons and Acts 1:15–26 *passim* (Easter 7B) narrates the selection of Matthias to fill out the number of the twelve disciples. The community of the baptized is enlivened by the multiplicity of the gifts of the Spirit (1 Cor 12:3b–7, 12–13; for Pentecost ABC). It is a community in-gathered and informed by the love of God (cf. the readings from 1 John).

Baptism and the attendant gift of the Holy Spirit pervade the selections from the New Testament appointed to be read in the season of Easter. The references to "initiation" motifs are so abundant that it is not possible within the confines of this essay even to catalog them all. The stupendous liturgical significance of the Great Vigil and the biblical witness' linking of the death and resurrection of Jesus and the baptism of believers must suffice as evidence that this is the principal controlling thematic development of the whole pericope system for Easter in all three years.

If readers, exegetes, and preachers fail to take into account the liturgical context of the passages selected, we run the risk of developing an understanding of this pericope system as providing nothing more than a serialized history of nascent Christianity. In fact the whole series provides the biblical basis for the church's mystagogia. The purpose of these readings is not to provide the modern churchgoer with an elementary history of the early church. (This is the error in the Lutheran adaptation of the three-year lectionary that provides for reading a larger portion of the book of

Acts.) The lessons selected by the framers of the lectionary provide the biblical warrant and occasion for addressing the fundamental issues involved in life in the community of the resurrected Lord Jesus.

Having been buried and raised again as participants in the death and resurrection of Jesus, our lives are radically and permanently altered and our relationships with one another are qualitatively changed. People who have died and who live now in the new life of Jesus Christ, in this end of all the ages, continue to be confronted by the implications of this transformation through the mystagogical teaching and preaching of the community. Easter is the season most especially devoted to the renewal of our inquiry into the meaning and implications of the resurrection of the Lord for our life together as the church, the risen body of Christ, the sacrament of God's abiding presence in the world.

The Sacramentary

Eleanor Bernstein

The Season of Lent

Believers for close to 20 centuries now have been welcoming Lent as an old friend, year after Christian year. This most ancient of seasons so deeply rooted in Christian consciousness and observance strides into the routine of late-winter, early-spring days and bids one attend to its presence. Ashes, shades of purple, images of desert and temptation, fasting, prayer and almsgiving, restraint in music and decor—all are familiar reminders that the church is journeying once again toward Easter, toward font and banquet table. Lent's spirit perdures—in hearts, in households of faith, in communities of believers. Its echoes are heard in the stories of scripture, in the words of our prayer, in psalms and hymns.

In other chapters of this book, attention is given to those elements that express the spirit of our lenten observance—music, environment, art, ritual, gesture, preaching, and central to all of these, the lectionary. In the next pages, Lent as it is reflected in the *words* of our prayer from the rites and texts of the sacramentary will be examined.

The lectionary and sacramentary, as two cherished "prayer books" of the Christian community, structure our eucharistic prayer life. Telling and retelling stories of faith, responding in praise and thanksgiving, in sorrow and petition, twentieth century believers join their voices with those of their forebears. And over the centuries, those lenten texts have "gathered up" the unspoken prayer, the deep-felt sentiments of repentant hearts. With an eye toward Easter and the procession to the font, the praying church is especially mindful of those who prepare for baptism, and this consciousness reminds all of their need to renew promises of baptismal faithfulness.

> The *Constitution on the Liturgy* states that, "the twofold character of the lenten season is to be brought into great prominence," that is, its baptismal character and its penitential character (#109).

> It is most desirable that in the revision of the liturgy, Lent be returned to its noble simplicity and adapted to the understanding of the people, so that the less important aspects are seen in perspective, and the entire season regains its unique effectiveness. ("Commentary on General Norms for the Liturgical Year and the Calendar")

Preparing for the primary worship events of the Catholic community during this season (Ash Wednesday, the Sundays of Lent) will require a grasp of the overall tone of the season, its relationship to baptism and thus to the Triduum and Eastertime, and a sensitive ordering of the prayer texts in the sacramentary—all of this while taking into account "the nature and circumstances of each assembly . . . to bring about conscious, active, and full participation of the people" (*General Instruction on the Roman Missal*, #3).

Because the options provided during Lent are numerous, great effort may be required to achieve clarity and familiarity with the texts so that the community's prayer can be both richly textured and of one piece. Carefully chosen texts can result in a prayerful season that reflects a unity and integrity, a harmony and balance that will not only express, but foster genuine lenten prayer. To that end, a careful investigation of the many elements will be required.

There are basic decisions to be made regarding introductory rites (entry, greeting, penitential rite or rite of sprinkling, opening prayer); general intercessions; preface, eucharistic prayer and communion rite; concluding rites (blessing, recessional). But beyond these, further possibilities exist (when the elect are present) which allow alternative Mass texts, prayers for the rites of scrutiny and exorcism and the presentations.

Prelude: Marked with Ashes

Ash Wednesday marks the dramatic beginning of a 40-day season of preparation for the paschal feast. The Mass texts of the First Sunday of Lent, with vivid imagery of desert, fasting and temptations announce the season's message of sin, grace and the triumph of the new Adam, but it is the act of being signed with ashes that brings the Christian up short to hear again the Lord's call: "But now, now—it is the Lord who speaks—come back to me with all your heart, fasting, weeping, mourning" (Joel 2:12, reading I).

Those charged to enable the community to begin this season well, those who plan the liturgy of Ash Wednesday, should be mindful of that fundamental principle of the spiritual life from the scriptures: it is the *Lord* who calls to repentance, the one who is merciful, all tenderness and compassion, slow to anger, rich in graciousness. It is the Lord's action that precedes the efforts of the sinner to repent of sin and turn to a new life. Indeed, it is this grace-filled invitation that prompts the Christian to undertake the lenten works of prayer, fasting and almsgiving. The individual's transformation will be the fruit of openness to the call, an openness nurtured by prayer, a prayer strengthened by the asceticism of fasting and proving itself in good works.

On Ash Wednesday the Christian community declares its sinfulness. (But it is not a day for confessions and penance services—that day will come later in Lent.) This day marks the outset, the beginning of an annual journey in company with other Christians who have heard the same call to "return to the Lord," and with the elect, the mature catechumens who are preparing for Easter baptism. The Forty Days are a "sacrament" bearing grace. As the lenten preface puts it: "This great season of grace is your gift to your family. . . ."

While the Sundays of Lent actually give shape to the season (cf. chapter on the lectionary) and draw out the fundamental baptismal and penitential themes of the Christian life, this day of *beginning*, of launching, bears a power all its own. It is, perhaps, the one weekday other than Christmas when Catholics fill their churches, when special schedules are announced, when additional liturgies are scheduled for the faithful to receive ashes—that unambiguous sign of mortality and repentance.

The sacramentary states that the giving of ashes is not to be done apart from a service of the word, a directive not to be skipped for the sake of convenience. To neglect the word on this day is to continue the poor theology and pastoral practice that emphasizes that the sacraments and sacramentals of the church "give grace" automatically, with little regard for the personal responsibility to bring a ready heart and openness to the Lord's presence in the words and signs that comprise the day's ritual. Without that context, we risk taking the sacraments themselves as holy *things* and not as privileged encounters with the God of our salvation.

The scripture texts of the day orient the penitent to undertake the discipline of this season in a spirit of dependence on the Lord, not neglecting the grace given in this "favorable time." The gospel teaching to do our lenten works "in secret" warns against a subtle spiritual pride that can destroy the good we will to do. Thus the proclamation of the scriptures and a brief homily should provide the context for the giving and receiving of ashes in a humble spirit. Having heard the word of God, the call to repentance, we sinners come forward and declare ourselves; we undertake this journey of renewal in preparation for the celebration of the Easter mysteries.

Whether the eucharist is to be celebrated or not, the introductory rites deserve careful attention. The worship space should obviously speak "Lent" as persons enter the church. The choice of appropriate music (instrumental or sung) is a high priority; music can set a tone in a way that little else can and express a spirit that enables prayer. After the gathering music, there is only the greeting and the opening prayer, since the penitential rite is omitted. The choice of the opening prayer should be in keeping with the emphasis of the homily, general intercessions and music selections.

In rendering the responsorial psalm, there is a distinct pastoral advantage to selecting one that will carry through the season. Psalm 51, designated for this day, is a solid "all purpose" lenten psalm. A good setting would be a valuable addition to the community's repertoire. Singing this same psalm during weekday and Sunday Masses can add just the right touch; the repetition through the weeks of Lent can unify the season and foster the lenten spirit of repentance and desire for the Lord's mercy. Likewise, the sung gospel acclamation.

The ritual of blessing and distribution of ashes is not a substitute for the homily. The rubrics of the sacramentary are clear: "*After the homily,* the priest joins his hands and says . . ." (italics added). Following the prayer of blessing, the ashes are sprinkled with holy water. The ashes, sign of death and of repentance; the cross, the paradox of life through death; the water, reminder of our baptismal passage through death come together here. When the faithful step forward to be signed with ashes in the form of a cross, they come forward to embrace a way of life that will lead to Easter glory, but a way of life already chosen in baptism that demands dying again and again in order to live more deeply the new life offered by Christ.

Two options are provided for giving the ashes: the old formula "Remember, you are dust . . ." and "Turn away from sin and be faithful to the gospel." The first obviously is a reminder of our mortality; the second, a straightforward call to conversion and gospel living. This latter reflects a spirituality more likely to resonate with church life of our times; it carries associations with the emphases of the RCIA and the challenge to pattern one's life on the teachings of the gospel.

The signing with ashes can be done by several ministers; these can surely be lay persons, and need not be restricted to eucharistic ministers. This is clarified in the January 1980 *BCL Newsletter*: "The minister for blessing ashes is always a priest or a bishop; other persons may be associated with the distribution—deacons, special ministers of communion and other lay persons where there is true pastoral need." It is advisable to involve persons who will be present for the entire liturgy in this ritual, rather than have priests and deacons appear for this part of the liturgy and then vanish again. To allow members of the assembly to assist affirms the basic belief that by reason of baptism all are called to minister to each other in this life-journey of conversion, both in word and in the witness of one's life.

During the signing, appropriate songs and psalmody may be sung or instrumental music played. In the early centuries, the practice of conferring ashes was reserved for those who declared themselves public penitents. One wonders if at least one effect of such a practice was to arouse prayerful sympathy within the community for the penitent. This sense of community should not be absent from our lenten observance; our common song and common sung prayer can foster the attitude that together we have received salvation from the Lord and are called as a *people* to return to him.

Following the giving of the ashes, the rite concludes with the general intercessions. The sample intercessions in the appendix of the sacramentary (Lent I and Lent II) are a good choice. Lent I is especially appropriate at the beginning of the season.

The text of the prayer over the gifts brings together the works of Lent, the celebration of the death/resurrection of Christ the Lord, the cleansing from sin and the renewal of spirit. Relating Lent and the paschal feast is an important element of the entire lenten observance and should not be overlooked.

The sacramentary recommends the fourth lenten preface (reward of fasting) for this day. The eucharistic prayers of reconciliation should be considered for use during Lent, with acclamations that by their musical setting support the spirit of lenten prayer. It would be wise to select at least one eucharistic acclamation that will serve as a sustaining element throughout the 40 days.

A familiar communion hymn or psalm response may accompany the communion rite, especially on this day when there is likely to be a larger number of communicants. While considerations of the length of the liturgy on a normal work day can't be ignored, the early morning or evening Masses will be attended by persons who are not free during the day. Those who make the extra effort to celebrate the liturgy on this day are justified in expecting a well-prepared worship experience, even within the on-the-way-to-work limits of 30 to 40 minutes.

The liturgy concludes with the prayer after communion, the blessing and dismissal. If singing has accompanied the communion rite, an instrumental may fittingly bring the liturgy to its end.

A prayerful Ash Wednesday liturgy goes a long way in helping believers to personally enter this season in the spirit of the church's lenten observance. The communal prayer experience, the ritual of the ashes, the familiar lenten readings and hymns provide the context out of which the journey of renewal and continuing conversion proceeds.

The Sundays of Lent: Primary Texts

Beginning Well—Introductory Rites

— Entrance, Greeting
— Penitential Rite or Sprinkling
— Opening Prayer

The primary purpose of the introductory rites is to *begin* the ritual celebration of the assembled faithful. Gathering the many into one through gesture, word and music so that they can become one heart, one voice in prayer is fundamental. Those who are familiar with the rites and know the intent will select and shape these initial elements so that they call forth the prayer of the assembly and prepare them to hear the word of the Lord.

This means achieving simplicity and focus, creating a tone of prayerfulness that is unmistakably lenten. More silence, fewer words, an environment for worship that suggests the season by use of color, texture, carefully chosen music and instrumentation, gestures—all of these can be externalizations of the spirit of Lent, an invitation to recommitment and a call to conversion. The decisions, then, that are made about the shape and texture of the beginning rites are quite significant.

Will the ministers process in? Will a hymn be sung by the whole assembly? Or will an antiphon be sung, choir/cantor and assembly alternating? Will instrumental music accompany the procession?

Perhaps a different style of "entrance" would serve well, with ministers taking their places, almost unobtrusively, in the sanctuary—deacon, presider, cantor, acolytes—as the people are taking their places in the pews. Instrumental music conducive to reflection can be played during this gathering time. As the hour for the liturgy approaches, one of the acolytes lights the candles, and the liturgy begins. Such a gathering time, well crafted, can be a strong call to worship and a striking sign of unity among those who gather as they prayerfully attend to the final preparation (an interior one) before celebrating the sacred mysteries. In such a model, the bearing and demeanor of the ministers seated in the sanctuary makes a strong statement. This is not the time for them to "check out" the assembly to see who's there; it is, rather, reflection time.

The greeting and the call to prayer should be straightforward; a lengthy introduction or commentary is rarely prayer and more often teaching. We are wise to let prayer be prayer, and its formative nature be just that.

The Kyrie or "Lord, have mercy" can be well used in this season as a processional litany or as the penitential rite. The sung repetition of the words either in Greek or in the vernacular can create an attitude of need for the Lord's mercy, a consciousness of one's desire for forgiveness that can be woven through the entire liturgy.

Options for the penitential rite are many: ministers and assembly kneeling in silence for a few moments and then praying the Confiteor; all kneeling during the singing of the Kyrie (or Lord, have mercy); form C of the rite with appropriate acclamations to Christ (numbers 1, 4 and 5 are among those in keeping with the lenten spirit; or, one may compose one's own). If this last is the choice, the litany should not be one of sins and omissions, e.g., "For the times we failed to . . ." This is not the meaning of form C, despite evidence of considerable confusion in this regard. The invocations acclaim the action and presence of the Lord on our behalf.

The rite of sprinkling is argued for during Lent by some, especially on the third Sunday, cycle A (gospel of the woman at the well), but the decision to use this may well confuse the tone of the lenten celebrations with that of Eastertime. If the sprinkling is chosen, it should be well integrated into the whole of the Sunday liturgy. In other words, one shouldn't make the choice just to add "a more positive note" to the experience of Lent. The time for blessing, baptizing and sprinkling water is the Easter Vigil; all of Lent moves toward this night of initiation.

This point about the rite of sprinkling in Lent bears on a larger question. How does one shape the introductory rites of any of the major seasons so that they fittingly speak of *this* season in word, gesture, music, movement? In other words, the beginning of the Sunday eucharist for the Second Sunday of Lent should not look or sound or feel like the beginning of the eucharist for the Thirteenth Sunday in Ordinary Time or like the Fourth Sunday in Eastertime. In planning the Sundays of Lent, the power of a consistent beginning should be aimed for—keeping the same shape, perhaps even the same music, throughout the season builds something familiar, gives unity to the season, and provides the community with a starting point for lenten prayer.

However one begins, simplicity is essential. "Less is more." If a litany or hymn is sung for the processional, it would be wise not to use a lengthy penitential rite, but something rather brief, and then to move directly to the opening prayer.

The opening prayer too often appears as an afterthought when the introductory rites are given a special shape. As the most important of the units that make up the introductory rites, the opening prayer should be for the assembly a gathering up of the unspoken prayer yet to be expressed. The text of that prayer should not go unexamined. The first option in the sacramentary is stated succinctly in the style of the classic Roman prayer forms; its directness and clear focus may well be the best choice in keeping with the overall tone of the season. The alternative opening prayers tend to be longer; often the phrasing and imagery are associated with a more contemporary style of religious expression and spirituality. In choosing the prayer, give attention to how "prayable" the text is. Often what seems acceptable in private reading, doesn't make "prayable prose." The best test is to read the prayer aloud, listening carefully to how it sounds. This attention to detail reflects a sensitivity to the words, sounds, rhythms and images of our prayer forms, and concern that these be avenues of access and not barriers to the mystery.

A final caution—the good liturgy is not one which is "letter perfect." Rather, it is one in which the community and the community's prayer has been served by the careful selection and the weaving together of music, text, movement, environment. The liturgist/planner doesn't manipulate prayer, but works with sensitivity to set free the Spirit of God in the heart of each believer and thus to enable prayer that is the Spirit's own utterance.

After the Word—General Intercessions

After the word of God has been proclaimed, after the homilist has broken that word for the nourishment of the faithful, and after some moments of quiet reflection, the assembly offers its prayer of intercession for the church, for the world, for those in special need, for the needs of the local community. Having heard once more the story of God's love for all peoples, the faithful respond in expressing concern for others. The prayer is an expansive one, not turned in on itself, but reaching beyond to the needs of the larger body, the body of Christ suffering, oppressed, lacking what is necessary for its well-being, both in spirit and in body.

Two sets of sample formulas for the lenten general intercessions are given in the appendix of the sacramentary (Lent 1, no. 5 and Lent 2, no. 6). These may be referred to as a guide, but need not be accepted as the only or the best examples of what may be done. Will the same intercessions be used each week? Will some of them be repeated? Will each Sunday have its own text? In addition to formulating the prayer text, thought needs to be given to *how* the prayer will be prayed. Spoken? Sung? Would a "Lord, have mercy" or "Lord, hear our prayer" in a simple or familiar musical setting best convey the tone of this season? How can this best be ritualized? What assists the *assembly's prayer* at this point in the liturgy and draws the faithful to the liturgy of the eucharist and the prayers at table?

Prayers at Table
— Prayer over the Gifts
— Preface
— Eucharistic Prayer and Acclamations

The gathering up of the money offering of the faithful and the bearing of the gifts of bread and wine to the altar table are a preparatory rite, not to be confused with what follows. And as the nature of any preparatory action (or rite) is subordinate to what is to come, the eucharistic celebration should reflect this ordering. After an extended word service (three scripture passages, psalm, homily, creed, general intercessions), one must ask what will best serve the prayer of the gathered community and the nature of the rite. Is the experience thus far one which needs another sung hymn by the assembly to "speak" something else? Does the assembly need more to reflect on, by way of a choir piece? Does the community need to come to rest, with silence or instrumental music as a transition between the liturgy of the word and the great prayer of thanksgiving about to begin? Often, this last option best suits the need and rhythm both of the liturgical act and of individual participants.

The prayer over the gifts is among the shortest of the propers in the sacramentary. It petitions a specific grace through the offering of the sacrifice. Since each Sunday and weekday of Lent has its own, no decisions or selections need to be made by the planners.

With the preface, on the other hand, there are a number of options. Lent I (the spiritual meaning of Lent) and Lent II (the spirit of penance) are provided for those lenten Masses, especially Sundays which have no preface of their own. The First and Second Sundays of Lent (cycles A, B, C) have designated prefaces that correspond to the gospel readings: the temptation on the first Sunday, the transfiguration on the second. There seems no reason to look for a preface other than these. On the third, fourth, and fifth Sundays of cycle A, specific prefaces are also given, again corresponding to the gospel passages: the woman of Samaria, the blind man, Lazarus. Since cycle A is recommended whenever a parish is preparing for the baptism of the elect at Easter, the prayer texts which underline these baptismal themes are wise choices. Indeed, cycle A may be used in any year (whether or not there are elect in the community) because of its clear focus on the meaning of Lent as a preparation for the celebration of the paschal mystery.

A number of *eucharistic prayers and acclamations* are acceptable. (Eliminate eucharistic prayer 4 from the outset, since it has its own preface.) Eucharistic prayers 1, 2, 3 as well as the eucharistic prayers of reconciliation are options. The latter may well serve the tone and movement of the lenten liturgies, with their emphasis on the saving life and actions of Jesus Christ and the community's thanksgiving for such a gift.

While the chapter on music deals with this subject in greater detail, it may be helpful to indicate here that there is value in keeping the same musical setting for the acclamations throughout this season and not changing from Sunday to Sunday. Repetition of text and melody can "identify" and give character to the season. Then, when the community moves into the festive celebration of Eastertime, a definite change in sound can signal the new time, with music expressive of the joy and new life of the Fifty Days.

After communion has been distributed, "all may sit for a period of silence, or a hymn or psalm may be sung" (*General Instruction,* #121). If a hymn has been sung during the communion procession, another hymn or psalm may seem too heavy or redundant here. A period of silence is most often welcomed as a time for reflecting on the gift given to the one and to the many—holy gifts for God's holy people. (Many parishes seem to err by allowing too little time for silence.) The prayer after communion is then offered.

Taking Leave
— Blessings, Prayers over the People
— Dismissal

When the communion rite is done, the remainder of the celebration should move to its conclusion. Necessary announcements can be made here before the final blessing and dismissal, but these should not give occasion for another homily, for moralizing, or for parish advertising.

The community is sent out with a *blessing.* Will the choice be the simple blessing? Or the prayers over the people? Or the solemn blessing? A solemn blessing is provided for each Sunday, although other texts may be chosen. Of the others included in the sacramentary, solemn blessing no. 5 (Passion of the Lord) is most appropriate. In determining which form to use during Lent, keep simplicity in mind, especially since the blessings for Eastertime could well be more expansive in keeping with a spirit of full celebration.

There are 24 *prayers over the people* which may be used on Sundays or feasts of the Lord. Refer to the suggestions for choosing the opening prayer in selecting among them. Ask: how does the text of this prayer "echo" the readings or the prayer of the celebration? Numbers 4, 6, 12, 14, 17, for example, reflect themes associated with Lent. Which is most suited to *this* Sunday in Lent?

And finally, the *dismissal* and recessional. Hymn? Instrumental music? Silence? Again, there are very fine possibilities, and the chapter on music in this book is a helpful guide. Don't use a hymn because that's "the only way to conclude," or because "that's what we've always done." One may opt for concluding every lenten eucharist the same way. A choice for consistency is not as important at the end of a celebration as at the beginning. What *is* important is sending this community to continue the lenten prayer, fasting, and good works that mark the life of the Christian in preparation for the paschal feast.

An Alternative: Mass Texts for Celebrating the RCIA

Special ritual Masses are provided for the rite of election and for the scrutinies. In these Mass texts, references are made to those preparing for baptism; the community petitions fitting graces for them as the time of their initiation draws near. In addition to the opening prayer, prayer over the gifts, and prayer after communion, an entrance antiphon for the three scrutinies (Ez 36:23-26) and communion antiphons taken from the gospels of those Sundays are provided. No special blessings are given.

Election or Enrollment of Names

When the rite of election is celebrated on the First Sunday of Lent, the inclusion of the catechumens (as well as other ministers to be involved) in the entrance procession should be given serious consideration. In this way, the presence of the catechumens is marked. They can be seated in prominent places with their godparents and families, and can again be recognized by parishioners as the new members that they are praying for and welcoming into the church community. Their presence need not alter the introductory rite as it has been planned for the lenten Masses. The Book of the Elect, however, may be carried in the procession and placed on a stand where the candidates will later inscribe their names during the rite of enrollment.

The rite itself includes five parts: the presentation, examination, admission or election, prayer for the elect, and dismissal. The bishop is the ordinary minister of the church who accepts candidates for baptism; however, for pastoral reasons, the rite of election is often held in the parish and the pastor (the bishop's delegate) presides. In other dioceses, a preparatory rite is celebrated at the Sunday parish eucharist before the diocesan rite of election. The chief catechist or coordinator of the RCIA can appropriately make the presentation, calling the candidates forward. They are accompanied by their godparents.

Note the distinction and interplay of roles within the community—bishop, pastor, catechist, godparents, assembly, immediate families of those to be enrolled. The ritual itself makes a statement about church and about life in the church, its development and dependence on a variety of gifts and an interplay of persons who, by their own commitment, support, nurture and witness to the power of the Spirit in the lives of this people.

What should be evident in any community is the witness of the church (i.e., the faithful) to the seriousness of this last step before initiation, their concern for the growth and development of the Christian spirit in these prospective members, and their intensified prayer for them. The words of the prayer texts (either as given or "in similar words"), the questions asked, the instructions given should be prayed and spoken with the sensitivity and understanding that convey the import of what is being done, without sounding moralistic.

The way the intercessory prayers are rendered can greatly contribute to the assembly's engagement in this element of the rite. When the intercessions are chanted and the response is sung, or sung over and over in mantra-style, the effect of the prayer can be powerful, providing an atmosphere or context that draws the rite to a conclusion and, at the same time, leaves echoes of the significance of what has just been witnessed.

The dismissal can take place simply. Once the new elect have gone out from the assembly, the liturgy continues as usual.

The Scrutinies

The scrutinies (third, fourth, fifth Sundays) are the church's continuing prayer "to purify the catechumens' minds and hearts, to strengthen them against temptation, to purify their intentions, and to make firm their decision, so that they remain more closely united with Christ and make progress in their efforts to love God more deeply" (RCIA, #154).

The elect may walk in procession and be seated with their god-parents and families. The texts of the prayers and the exorcisms, integrally linked to the gospel texts, further elucidate the implications of the word that has been proclaimed, not only for the elect, but for the entire community. The prayer intensifies throughout the lenten Sundays, as Christ the living water, Christ the light, Christ the true life confronts the believers. The use of gestures (kneeling or bowing in the case of the elect, touching, laying on of hands) strongly embodies the spoken or sung prayer.

While the presider is the one designated in the ritual to lay hands on the elect, the gesture need not be limited to him, but may also involve others who have had roles in the initiation process, as well as the godparents. Perhaps at the first scrutiny, only the presider; at the second, presider and ministers; at the third, presider, ministers and godparents, to express a progressive involvement and intensity as the days of final preparation draw to a close. This laying on of hands, done reverently and without haste, (preferably in silence) is a dramatic liturgical gesture.

The same suggestion offered for the intercessions in the rite of election applies here. See the several options in the text of the RCIA; these are not included in the sacramentary.

Passion (Palm) Sunday

While the first five Sundays of Lent develop as an unfolding preparation for the celebration of the paschal mystery of the Lord's death and resurrection, Passion (Palm) Sunday is almost an interruption in the lenten Sunday rhythm, with its blessing of palms, procession, and proclamation of the passion narrative. The liturgy is, in fact, a hybrid, the ritual of the palms (blessing and procession) being grafted onto a Sunday eucharist that included from very early times a proclamation of the passion. At one point in the historical evolution of this observance, there were two Sundays: one designated Passion Sunday; the other, Palm Sunday.

Now that the two have been brought together, a difficulty arises. How does one bring together into one liturgy the "glad hosannahs" and the cries, "Crucify him!" There is a radical shift in the mood of the celebration once we begin the liturgy of the word. The planning is easier if one remembers some basics about proper emphasis and subordination of the various elements.

In the renewed liturgy, the blessing of the palms and the procession have been simplified. The simplification hints at what we are about on this last Sunday before Easter: it is *the passion narrative* which holds the priority. And within the palm ritual, the emphasis should be on Jesus' entry into Jerusalem as the messiah. Adrian Nocent sees the blessing of palms as secondary, and the *procession* as primary.

> In this procession we are to see much more than a mimetic reminder; we are to see the ascent of God's people, and our own ascent, with Jesus to the sacrifice. . . . If we were to see in the procession only a crowd waving palms and singing joyous songs, we would miss its real significance in the Roman liturgy. That liturgy looks upon the procession not simply as a commemoration of Christ's entry into Jerusalem nor simply as a triumphal march, but as Christ's journey, together with his people, to Calvary and the great central act of redemption. (*The Liturgical Year*, vol. 2: *Lent and Holy Week*, p. 195)

Thus, this Sunday which stands at the head of the week that includes the celebration of the Triduum has an important role for the Christian community. It situates the liturgy of these coming holy days: it is the *church* that enters into the Triduum, making that passage with her Lord. Friday, Saturday, Sunday are not historical flashbacks of what happened to Jesus; neither are they an annual pilgrimage back to first century Palestine to *be there* at the important events of salvation. Rather, each year the whole church enters into this celebration of the paschal mystery, proclaiming the life-giving death of Jesus, dying with him in order to lay hold of life at a deeper level—especially in those who will enter the death-resurrection waters of baptism at the Vigil. Palm Sunday images that; we go up to Jerusalem to suffer and die, that we may also rise with him.

Some practical considerations. To begin with, have enough palms or branches so that every person will have one. The palm, symbol of victory, is also sign of the Christian's hope in the face of death. Often parishioners bring their own branches of evergreen, but additional branches should be available at the church. Ideally the blessing takes place away from the church, in a courtyard, patio or hall, and the faithful process into the church singing hymns to their victorious Lord. The movement, the processing, is not dispensable in light of the preceding discussion. Procession means moving from one place to another, going somewhere—not just leaving one's pew, going up and down the aisles of the church and returning to the same place. The solemn blessing and procession (first form) should be used whenever possible—even at more than one liturgy. However, pastoral practice may tell us that only one major procession is appropriate—even as we keep only once in each community the liturgies of the Triduum. When there is to be no procession involving the assembly, the following "adaptation" may serve well. The presider comes into the sanctuary as the assembly sings a suitable hymn or antiphon. After the greeting, the introduction and prayer, he walks through the assembly sprinkling the palms held by the faithful and remains at the rear of the church. The gospel is proclaimed from the rear of the church if possible; the assembly turns to follow the procession to the sanctuary.

Admittedly, this is not the same as walking from the courtyard or across the church grounds into the church itself. But such an option (or something similar) eliminates the purposeless walking around the church or no movement at all. Liturgy planners must take the limits and possibilities of their own space into account and work from there, mindful of what this liturgy of Palm Sunday is about.

The remaining choices of prayers, blessings, etc. are governed by principles already laid out in the section on lenten Sundays.

Eastertime: The Great Sunday

Following the lenten prayer, fasting, and almsgiving, the church enters into the glorious Fifty Days, the Great Sunday (seven weeks of seven days), characterized by Easter alleluias, feasting and celebrating in the community that has been disciplined, nurtured and given new members in the living waters of the font.

The Sundays of Eastertime, which conclude on the 50th day after the resurrection of the Lord, Pentecost Sunday, should explode with the deep joy of those who have, indeed, passed through death and come to new life. In these Sundays of Easter, as in the lenten Sundays, a unity of theme and spirit should be obvious, reflected in the music, in the environment for worship, in the prominence of the Easter symbols: the paschal candle and the font. *A community may* have the newly baptized (the neophytes) keep their special places at the front of the assembly during this season, the time of mystagogy. They may also participate as gift bearers.

The fullness of the eucharistic sign (bread and cup for all) shouldn't be forgotten until next year's Triduum. Fresh flowers, plants, altar cloths, vesture, candles and incense—care for all of these reflects a consciousness of the "new day" that is the risen Christ, the one who has opened up a gathering place for the people redeemed in his blood.

In keeping festival for 50 days, we take time to dwell in the mystery of the Lord's life-from-death-experience (which is also our own), each Sunday drawing out another facet of that mystery. The Sundays of Easter, then, all seven of them, shouldn't become like the Ordinary Time Sundays after the second week. How they will continue to echo the Easter Vigil–Easter Sunday celebration will require thoughtful planning. The temptation to coast in these weeks of Easter after the demands of Lent and the Triduum would betray the spirit of Lent–Eastertime. We are called to "praise God with greater joy than ever in this Easter season, when Christ became our paschal sacrifice" (Easter preface). Indeed, to take for granted these Sundays of Easter would be to distort the Christian mystery itself. The discipline, fasting, asceticism of Lent is purposeful, not masochistic; it is to fine tune us once again to live the Christian life fully. It is that life we rejoice in and celebrate in this paschal season.

A New Beginning

— Entrance, Greeting
— Rite of Sprinkling
— Glory to God
— Opening Prayer

The entrance rite in Eastertime should clearly sound the Easter note. Processions should be festive—perhaps including the neophytes on some Sundays—amidst alleluias and Easter hymns or psalms. Candles, incense, the victorious cross, as well as the gospel book should be borne proudly through the assembly. A "festive" entrance rite does not mean the rite should be overly long, making the celebration top heavy. Its function is still to provide a *beginning*.

The rite of sprinkling, most appropriately used in this season, is probably the single best sign of the continuing celebration of Easter, and as such can be a reminder of the Vigil and a thread linking all of the Sundays to the Vigil and to each other. But because the rite of sprinkling involves an additional text of blessing as well as movement through the assembly, be especially sensitive to the structuring of the rites so as not to make the opening unwieldy.

One option that works well is using the Glory to God as the entrance hymn. The setting must be one for which the assembly can sing the refrain, the cantor/choir sing the verses. Avoid a setting that is sung by the choir alone. A sung Gloria can begin the celebration on a festive note and lead smoothly into the sprinkling rite.

The sacramentary provides a special text (form C) for the blessing of water during the Easter season; however, the directive allows for "using these or similar words." The presider who composes his own blessing would do well to note the scriptural references and images used in the sacramentary and craft his own in that light. The blessing of the water and the sprinkling are important gestures. If there is no baptismal pool, then provision for a very large container should be made. Perhaps the water can be slowly poured from a handsome pitcher during the blessing. The vessels chosen and the way they are used and handled make a statement about the dignity of baptism. Using an evergreen branch of spruce, cedar or pine to sprinkle the water speaks life. And natural branches are more efficient than metal aspergilla! Take note of the advice in *Environment and Art in Catholic Worship*:

> All . . . vessels and implements used in the liturgical celebration should be of such quality and design that they speak of the importance of the ritual action. Pitchers, vessels for holy oils, bowls, cruets, sprinklers, censers, baskets for collection, etc.—all are presented to the assembly in one way or another and speak well or ill of the deed in which the assembly is engaged. (#97)

The movement of the presider through the assembly (perhaps one or two other ministers will move down the side aisles if the church is large) should allow *all*, not just a token few, to experience the rite—to see and feel the water. The use of a psalm or the repetition of a psalm verse is recommended; it is essential that the assembly participate. The rite is awkward when the assembly remains passive; it becomes a "waiting time" until the ministers return to their places and continue the celebration. Guard against having the faithful merely "sung to" and "sprinkled on" or else the liturgy will seem to have stopped before it has started. The rite concludes with the absolution.

If *the Gloria* has not been used as the processional, it is sung now. It is a hymn of praise; Eastertime is no time to settle for a droned recitation. Nor should the assembly be content to let the choir sing their praise for them.

The texts of the options for *the opening prayer* differ greatly; determine beforehand which one is pastorally and theologically suited to the community. Read the prayer aloud, listening to the rhythm of the words and the phrasing, not only to the thought content. In these early years of a vernacular liturgy, we do well to attend to the *sound* of our prayer texts. Unfortunately, some don't "read" well, and that discovery often isn't made until one hears the prayer aloud.

Let Us Pray—General Intercessions

The sacramentary provides only one formula for the general intercessions during the Easter season. The petitions include images of the Good Shepherd, the peace and joy associated with Easter, witnessing to Christ's resurrection. They provide insight into the consciousness of the church in this post-resurrection time. Other options may be to include a prayer for the neophytes in one's own community as well as all church communities, to pray for warring nations, to remember those who will be receiving initiation sacraments during this season (first eucharist, confirmation, others to be baptized), for those who are preparing to marry this spring and summer. It is still "in season" to pray that the community appropriate and give witness to the paschal mystery in their lives. Should the intercessions be chanted and the response sung, use a different setting from that used in Lent to mark the uniqueness of this season.

Using the same set of intercessions throughout Eastertime shouldn't be considered an easy way out. If the intercessions are well written and provide the community with a prayer that embraces the church and the whole human family and its needs, then the very repetition of them in a prayerful mode may enable a new experience of intercessory prayer.

Continual change rather than consistency in some of the elements of liturgy "robs" the ritual of its power to be prayer for many. Perhaps in the major church seasons, we would do well to maintain more of the constant and allow for repetition (a primary characteristic of ritual prayer) to make its impact.

Giving Thanks . . . with Greater Joy

— Prayer over the Gifts
— Preface
— Eucharistic Prayer and Acclamations
— Communion Rite

The table liturgy of the Easter season should certainly not be "back to the usual." Baptism finds its fulfillment at the table; it is the reason we bring members to the font, the reason they are anointed and clothed in white garments—so that they can gather at the banquet table of the kingdom. The liturgy of the eucharist, then, deserves the careful planning that will reflect this consciousness—that, indeed, it is the center, the Christian's life source, the sign par excellence of appropriating the paschal mystery. If this is our stance, then we can hardly do with less than the fullness of the eucharistic sign: bread and wine for all.

Whatever is done musically during *the preparation of the table and gifts* should not overpower the eucharistic prayer. The subordination of the preparatory rite is fundamental to the rhythm of the liturgy. No surprise that the preface and eucharistic prayer with acclamations fade into insignificance in the experience of many and are experienced as a "time between" homily and the reception of communion, if the preparation rite is used for elaborate choir pieces.

If *the preface* is not sung, a good musician may be able to provide simple accompaniment as the presider prays the prayer that heads into the Holy. String instruments (guitar, Celtic harp, dulcimer), or keyboard (piano, organ) can create a unifying context for the prayer, drawing presider and assembly together, weaving the spoken text and the sung acclamation together harmoniously.

Five Easter prefaces are given: Easter I (paschal mystery) to be used at the Vigil, on Easter Sunday and during the octave; Easter II (new life in Christ); Easter III (Christ lives and intercedes for us forever); Easter IV (the restoration of the universe through the paschal mystery); Easter V (Christ is priest and victim). Choices should be made in keeping with the overall spirit of the liturgy, with attention to the scriptures of the day. The same is true of the eucharistic prayer and the acclamations. There is liturgical wisdom in selecting one of the acclamations for use throughout the season, with a setting that sings "Easter life-from-death."

As a sign of our being risen with Christ, it may be well to consider standing during *the eucharistic prayer* throughout the season. This is certainly not an innovation:

> The principal posture (aside from the early period with its meal celebration) has always been a posture of standing. Before the higher Being whom he wishes to honor, a person stands erect, particularly when he realizes his obligation of service. Just as the priest at the altar stands before God in reverential readiness, so also the faithful; they are the *circumstantes*. (Joseph A. Jungmann, *The Mass of the Roman Rite*, p. 172.)

Standing also identifies the assembly with the presider praying in its name, and may help to emphasize that the prayer he gives voice to is the prayer of the whole body.

The Easter season is an acceptable time for communities to give attention to *the communion rite*. How can the breaking of the bread and the sharing of bread and cup be raised to a level of prayerful ritual that expresses and communicates the meaning of Christian life as a sharing in the body of the Lord? Admittedly, our fast-food style of life wars against gracious dining. But perhaps this is another reason why the rituals of the Christian assembly need to be taken so seriously—to counter a way of life that all too frequently disregards what is valuable, respectable and precious in human existence.

The communion rite and singing go together despite the baggage we bring to the new liturgy from our pre-Vatican II experience, a kind of "Jesus-and-I" spirituality. However, the use of music at communion time has been difficult to implement; often weary music directors and liturgists have settled for a choir piece or an instrumental. What seems to work best (and this requires time to take root in the community) is the use of a psalm with an antiphon that the assembly can repeat, or a eucharistic hymn such as "Gift of Finest Wheat" (now included in the repertoire of almost every Roman Catholic parish in the United States), with a recurring antiphon. The point is that singing together helps us grow in the consciousness that communion means not just union with the Lord, but union with his body, the church; this is essential to a solid eucharistic theology and ecclesiology.

After communion and a time for silent prayer, the choir and/or assembly may sing an Easter hymn, joyously bringing to a conclusion the mystery celebrated. The presider prays the final prayer and then offers the blessing.

Going in Peace

Solemn blessings are given for each of the Sundays of Easter. If, in the lenten season, one has opted for simpler, shorter texts, then this form of the blessing during these 50 days is a strong contrast. The text, even in its form, is expansive and thus expressive of the fullness of Easter joy, peace, and expectation.

One would not expect to sing a recessional if an Easter hymn was sung after communion. A fine organ piece accompanying the ministers and the faithful as they leave the assembly makes a dramatic ending.

Ascension

The solemnity of the Ascension of the Lord is a rather straightforward celebration. Recognizing the Lord's return to the Father, the church is charged to "make disciples of all nations" (Mt 28:19).

The prayer texts remind us of the new creation where Christ is and the "place" he has prepared for us: "May we follow him into the new creation" (opening prayer); "May his gift help us rise with him to the joys of heaven" (prayer over the gifts); "Help us to follow Christ with love to eternal life" (prayer after communion).

An essential piece of theology is hidden away in the final prayer: "In this eucharist we touch the divine life you give the world." Essential—lest we make the mistake of acting as though the "new creation" is in some unearthly, otherworldly realm: "Why do you stand here looking up at the skies?" (Acts 1:11)

The homily and general intercessions can highlight what is central to this feast, and move away from the nostalgic and sentimental. Needless to say, snuffing out the paschal candle is no longer part of the ritual. The candle remains visible and should be lit throughout the Easter season which concludes on Pentecost Sunday.

Because this is a weekday liturgy, time limits can't be ignored. Nevertheless, as a feast of the Lord, it should be celebrated well, with appropriate attention given to music, environment and to the liturgy of the word.

Pentecost

The preface for Pentecost expresses a theology of this feast that can serve well as the basis for liturgy planning:

> Today you sent the Holy Spirit
> on those marked out to be your children
> by sharing the life of your only Son,
> and so you *brought the paschal mystery to its completion.*
> (italics added)

> Today we celebrate the beginnings of your Church
> when the Holy Spirit made known to all peoples
> the one true God,
> and created from the many languages . . .
> one voice to profess one faith.

> The joy of the resurrection renews the whole world,
> while choirs of heaven sing for ever to your glory.

Pentecost Sunday concludes the Great Sunday, 50 days of paschal celebration of the mystery of Jesus Christ's victorious and life-giving death and resurrection. That mystery comes to fulfillment in the gift of the Spirit that draws many peoples, many languages into one voice, professing one faith. That same Spirit continues "to work in the world through the hearts of all who believe" (opening prayer, Mass during the day).

Thus the feast is a culmination; it is a celebration of the church called into being by Jesus Christ through the working of the Holy Spirit. It is a celebration of unity and of gospel mission. The scripture texts are rich and provide many options for the homily; numerous music selections offer a wide range of choice.

Consider what will best express the link between Easter and Pentecost. By the use of the rite of sprinkling, by wise selection of prayer and hymn texts, and by careful preparation of the general intercessions, associations between this feast and the Easter celebration can be drawn out, leading the faithful to rejoice in the gift that is given to enable the mission of all the baptized.

The sequence which the rubrics indicate is not to be omitted. It is poetry, and rendered best in a musical setting. It is probably awkward as a lengthy word-piece after a first reading, psalm and second reading. It may serve well as a choir piece before the liturgy begins, or as a meditative reflection following the homily or during the preparation of gifts. If it is to be included within the liturgy of the word, it may accompany an extended and festive gospel procession. Don't eliminate the possibility of using the Latin chant setting for a touch of the old and familiar.

Scheduling baptisms on this day is most appropriate (cf. the Vigil Mass for Pentecost, with its many readings paralleling the Easter Vigil).

One of the primary hymns used at Easter is a good choice on this day as an obvious conclusion of the Great Sunday, the community having come full circle in its observance of the paschal season. There is no need to use several languages in the liturgy (as at the general intercessions or the proclamation of the readings). We may by such practices be compromising the primary symbols— baptismal sprinkling, the paschal candle, the proclaiming of the word, the sharing of bread and cup. Let these stand out by reason of their being done well—central symbols of the faith professed by the whole church.

For the newly baptized, the neophytes, Pentecost concludes the period of mystagogy. They now take their places within the community to carry on the mission of the church. A community may decide to invite them all to the same liturgy, to include a prayer for them in the general intercessions, and then to host a Pentecost party. (See the RCIA, #237.) Mark the end of this period of the RCIA and of the church's paschal season with a community gathering.

The Rites of Initiation

Richard Fragomeni

A few years ago, I was invited to a parish to speak at a liturgical ministers' gathering. Before the keynote, I met a woman who touched me deeply. She asked me who I was, what I would be doing, and if it would be any good. I responded that I was the keynote speaker, that I was speaking about liturgy and music, and that I would do my best. Gazing wide-eyed at me she concluded the exchange by pointing her finger to my forehead—a la E.T.—and saying: "To do the best you can, Father, that's what saints are made of!" I agree.

We liturgists, musicians and catechists along with presbyters, deacons and other parish leaders are called to do the best we can. This is especially true when it comes to the Lent and Easter seasons and to the celebrations of the RCIA. To this end this article will explore the rites of the catechumenate that take place during these 90 days set aside each year to celebrate church membership and mission.

A word of caution: what follows is neither a recipe for instantaneous success nor the final word about the rites. Rather, it summarizes what can be done, what has been happening, and some current pastoral questions about the periods of enlightenment and mystagogia and their celebrations.

The Period of Enlightenment: Lent
Ash Wednesday

Lent is ushered in on Ash Wednesday. The baptized come forward and receive ashes to acknowledge their willingness to be renewed.

Their lenten journey, symbolized by the reception of ashes, takes place in a full assembly with those who are preparing for baptism and full communion with the church at the Easter Vigil.

The Ash Wednesday ritual's obvious connection with penance, a process of re-initiation, raises an important question for a parish catechumenate team: should the catechumens and candidates for full communion (from now on referred to here as candidates) come forward for the sprinkling with ashes? Let us be clear on this point. If being signed with ashes is a sincere gesture of repentance and renewal of the baptized, it is inappropriate for either catechumens or candidates to receive ashes. A parish might consider, however, dismissing the catechumens and candidates after the signing with ashes so that those preparing for initiation might experience the solidarity of the lenten retreat with the faithful. This connection needs to be made by the homilist at the celebration. The dismissal would follow as usual before the general intercessions. In any case, this issue should be considered before the Ash Wednesday celebration.

The First Sunday of Lent: The Rite of Election

For the catechumens and candidates, the First Sunday of Lent marks the turning point of their journey. The "rite of election or enrollment of names" is celebrated. Summoned to prayer and renewal on Ash Wednesday, the catechumens and candidates come forward to have the church publicly acknowledge their response to God's call. The RCIA makes a strong statement about the readiness of the person before this is celebrated:

> Before the election is celebrated, the candidates are expected to have a conversion of mind and conduct, a sufficient acquaintance with Christian teaching, and a sense of faith and charity. A decision on their suitableness is also required. Later, in the actual celebration of the rite, the manifestation of their intention and the decision of the bishop or his delegate should take place in the presence of the community. It is thus clear that election, which enjoys such a great solemnity, is the turning point of the whole catechumenate. (#23)

Two pastoral-liturgical considerations need to be explored: where the rite of election is celebrated and how it is celebrated appropriately.

The rite of election is presided over by the bishop or his delegate. This assumes that it takes place on a diocesan level and most likely at the cathedral church. A cathedral celebration certainly emphasizes the ecclesial significance of the event. Imagine hundreds of catechumens and candidates from an entire diocese gathered around the diocesan bishop, filling the cathedral. The gathering says: "Something *big* is happening." The something "big" is obviously the official proclamation that these catechumens and candidates, "the elect," are ready for initiation into the Catholic community.

Let us return to our first question. The cathedral setting gives a wider sense of church to election. The celebrations and catechesis of the catechumenate have been taking place in the parish community. Now the bishop, at the cathedral, enters at this turning point to mediate the call of God and receive the response of the elect. He officially proclaims the lenten days of prayer and fasting to be a retreat for the whole diocese in preparation for the Easter sacraments. A pastoral question has surfaced about the role of the parish community in election on the First Sunday of Lent. Aren't they cut off from one of the key moments of the initiation process if election is celebrated in a diocesan setting? To solve this problem many dioceses throughout North America have a two-phased celebration that begins in the parish church and culminates at the cathedral. The parish celebration acknowledges the local community and its role throughout the catechumenate. The cathedral celebration points to the broader reality of the church universal. This dual location of the rite works. It brings us to the second concern. How is election celebrated appropriately, so that the parish and cathedral rites do not duplicate each other?

Many diocesan offices working with the RCIA assist parishes by coordinating the two rites and sending parishes outlines and planning aids for both the parish and cathedral rites.

PARISH CELEBRATION

A rite for the parish follows the basic pattern of service from the RCIA. A designated parish celebration is set aside for the rite and announced in advance to the assembly. The catechumens and candidates enter in procession at the gathering rite. They are greeted by the presider and the assembly; the focus of the celebration is proclaimed. The sacramentary provides proper prayers for the occasion, which are used in place of those for the First Sunday of Lent. These are found in the ritual section. The opening prayer is:

> God our Father,
> you always work to save us,
> and now we rejoice in the great love
> you give to your chosen people.
> Protect all who are about to become
> your children, and continue to bless
> those who are already baptized.

The liturgy of the word takes place as usual, with the readings of the proper cycle. The election rite begins after the homily. What takes place at this point in the celebration will be complemented at the cathedral rite. The catechumens and candidates are called forward with their sponsors and stand near the presider. The sponsors are asked to testify briefly on behalf of those they are sponsoring. This testimony would be prepared by each sponsor and indicate the ways these persons have been responding to God's call along their journey of faith. Following the testimony, the assembly could give its assent to the readiness of the catechumens and candidates by further, spontaneous testimony. This could be done from the pews. Mention then would be made of the cathedral celebration.

The parish Book of the Elect, well designed and bound, is brought forward. The candidates and catechumens approach the book and sign it. Their sponsors and the presider do the same. An appropriate acclamation is sung as a public proclamation of God's call and these persons' response. The public calling of the names at this point may be omitted, since they will be called at the cathedral liturgy.

The prayers over the elect are now prayed and then the elect are dismissed. Led out by a catechist, holding the Book of the Elect, they gather in an appropriate place for reflection and shared prayer. For the assembly, the eucharist follows. At the end of the eucharist, all are invited to attend the cathedral celebration.

If there is time before leaving for the cathedral, candidates and catechumens could enjoy a meal together with their families and pray together in anticipation of the cathedral rite.

CATHEDRAL RITE

What would then happen at the cathedral to complete the celebration? At the cathedral that same day (or during that next week) the candidates and catechumens gather from all the parishes of the diocese with their sponsors, catechists, presbyters and parish communities. They bring the Book of the Elect that has been signed at the parish.

After the gathering song, the bishop welcomes the church and prays the opening prayer. Readings are carefully chosen for this rite. The readings from the morning celebration are not repeated.

The bishop then shares a homily in which he explains the importance of the rite of election for the whole church. He links the journey of the elect with the lenten journey of the faithful. Following his words, the celebration reaches its highpoint. One by one, parish representatives (usually the director of the catechumenate) come forward and call the names proudly, first of the catechumens, then of the candidates. This distinction is to be clear when the names are given. These elect now come forward, parish by parish, and present their Book of the Elect to the bishop. A musical acclamation could be used to punctuate the calling of names.

When all have been called and the books received by the bishop, he questions the elect about their intention to continue responding to God's call. He asks for the approval of the sponsors and the assembly.

The Books of the Elect, having been arranged in appropriate baskets or trays, are raised high by the bishop and the deacons for all to see. With the books raised, the bishop proclaims robustly: "These are the names of those who are now the elect—and who will this Easter Vigil be initiated into our community." An acclamation of praise is sung! Begin the acclamation right on time—like electricity at the heels of the bishop's proclamation. Sloppy timing, or an acclamation unfamiliar to the assembly could distort this whole action.

Following the proclamation of the names, the prayers for the elect are prayed and the closing blessing is given. In the prayers for the elect, petitions might include remembrance of the other Christian churches that nourished the faith of the candidates preparing for full communion at Easter.

The rite of election in these two complementary parts would look like this in outline form:

Parish Rite
- Gathering song
- Introduction and focusing words
- Liturgy of the word
- Homily
- Presentation of candidates and catechumens
- Testimony of sponsors
- Testimony of the assembly
- Signing of names in the Book of the Elect
- Prayer over the elect
- Dismissal
- Eucharist

Cathedral Rite
- Gathering song
- Introduction and words of welcome
- Liturgy of the word (readings selected especially for the occasion)
- Homily by bishop
- Calling of the names of catechumens and candidates by a parish representative
- Presentation of Books of the Elect to the bishop
- Questioning of the elect
- Questioning of sponsors and assembly
- Proclamation of election
- Prayer for the elect
- Closing rites
- Reception and meeting the bishop

A closing word. Diocesan offices that coordinate the catechumenate and the rite of election could keep a record of the names, parishes and home addresses of those elected. The bishop could easily write a letter of congratulation and invite each of them to the Mass with the neophytes to be celebrated during the Easter season.

The Three Scrutinies

The purpose of the scrutinies is twofold: "to teach the catechumens gradually about the mystery of sin, from which the whole world and each person desire to be redeemed, and thus be saved from its present and future effects; . . . to fill their minds with the meaning of Christ the redeemer." (RCIA, #157)

The process of liberation that is celebrated in the scrutinies is a mystery infinitely incomprehensible. "Scrutiny" means "a deep hard look at something." Using the cycle A readings as the normative texts for these rites, the elect are asked with the entire assembly to take a deep look at their thirsts (Samaritan woman), their blindness (blind man), and their decay (Lazarus). With the community, the elect pray for deliverance from these evils.

Theologians and liturgists are presently struggling with the scrutinies because they raise significant questions about the nature of evil. Are we praying in these rites for the forgiveness of personal sin and asking for exorcism from the evil that we ourselves have created as a result of our own actions, or lack of action? Or, on the other hand, are we seeking for deliverance from more global evil—social sin that we inherit by birth into it. The focus of the scrutinies seems to be God's deliverance of the community from a more social dimension of evil.

These celebrations, then, are mighty in scope. No wonder they are the least celebrated of the rites of the RCIA. They sting. When celebrated with power they can engage the whole community—not only the elect—in taking a deep, hard look into the mystery of iniquity. We face our helplessness in the face of evil and celebrate God's power to save us from being dominated by it.

How does a parish celebrate these rites significantly? The basic outline of the rite is this:

- Proclamation of scripture
- Homily
- Invitation to prayer
- Intercessions for the elect
- Exorcism
  - Part I – Prayer
  - Laying on of hands
  - Part II – Prayer
- Dismissal of the elect

This is the bare structure of a profound herald of God's liberation. The outline needs flesh and breath. Here are some possible directions.

Consider creating a litany of deliverance. This litany could be composed by the elect themselves at a catechetical session. It would petition for freedom from the evils that hold us back from being all we can be for the life of the world. Parish musicians could then add a musical setting to the litany, and the assembly could sing a response to the tropes. This litany would make a powerful gathering song on one of the scrutiny Sundays. New tropes could be added each week of the scrutinies to show the continuity of the rites of liberation.

Consider inviting the entire assembly to kneel with the elect in praying for the healing power of God. On one of the Sundays, the entire congregation might also extend their hands toward the elect as the presider lays hands on them in silence. On all three Sundays, the sponsors should lay their hands on the elect—the rubric says "on their right shoulder." Perhaps this could be adapted to "on their heads" while the presider prays the exorcism prayers.

One interesting adaptation that needs further critical reflection is the practice of inviting the elect to stretch out their hands over the assembly while the presider prays another prayer of exorcism over the congregation. This would take place after the exorcism prayers have been prayed over the elect. This practice is meant to show how the assembly, ever in need of renewal, is ministered to by the elect and their example of conversion. This custom, however, raises more issues of liturgical significance, and should be considered more deeply before used.

In any case, the scrutinies are simple rites with a lot of power. The key elements are: the proclamation of the word, the intensity of the homily, the gestures of kneeling, laying on of hands, the silence, the prayer. The symbolic nature of these rites can move an entire assembly profoundly.

Two pastoral issues have surfaced about the scrutinies. First, what readings should be used when the scrutinies are celebrated each year? The RCIA is quite clear that the three readings from cycle A are to be used. "The first Mass of the scrutinies is always that of the Samaritan woman, the second of the man born blind, and the third of Lazarus" (RCIA, #159). Some have suggested that all three cycles be used instead. This would give a complete set of readings to the assembly who may never hear the B or C cycles.

Some have encouraged this adaptation and adapted the exorcism prayers. While this is an excellent example of cultural and pastoral adaptation of the rite, this author believes that the power of the A cycle readings cannot be replaced by the B and C cycles. One cannot tire, it seems to me, of the genius of symbol in these stories from John's gospel. This is an area of unfinished business in the liturgical discussion of the RCIA.

Liturgy planners should note the proper prayers, prefaces and interpolations for the eucharistic prayers that are to be used when the scrutinies take place. These are found in the ritual Mass section of the sacramentary. These prayers are a thread of continuity throughout the entire rite.

A second pastoral concern is that of the appropriateness of including in the scrutinies the candidates (those already baptized in another Christian community). This needs lengthy discussion. Suffice for now to say: Yes, include them. Take care that the language used to introduce and refer to the elect distinguishes the two groups. The important notion is that all people need continual deliverance from the social evil that influences our behavior and thoughts. The scrutinies call the whole community to seek God's freedom from these dominating forces.

The Presentations

The RCIA celebrates two presentations: the presentation of the creed and the presentation of the Lord's Prayer.

The presentation of the creed is ordinarily celebrated during the week after the first scrutiny. It can also be celebrated during the catechumenate period. The celebration consists in handing on the creed to the elect. The creed is memorized by them and recited publicly on Holy Saturday morning. Both for this rite and for the presentation of the Lord's Prayer, the reader is directed to the book *The Rites of Christian Initiation* by Michel Dujarier (New York: Sadlier, 1979) for an excellent background for planning the presentations.

The presentation of the Lord's Prayer is usually placed during the week after the third scrutiny. A parish might also celebrate it during the catechumenate period, or it may be left for the preparatory rites of Holy Saturday morning.

Since these rites are given secondary importance in the RCIA, the caution is not to make them primary. Some parishes and dioceses celebrate the presentations on the Sundays of Lent instead of the scrutinies. This practice is *not* appropriate. Another practice has been to celebrate the presentations by the bishop at the cathedral instead of the rite of election or in conjunction with the election. This is an inappropriate adaptation both pastorally and liturgically. Every effort should be made to keep what is central, central.

The Dismissal Rite on Sundays and during the Triduum

The RCIA uses the word *dismissal* a great deal. Not only during Lent but during the entire catechumenate, the candidates and catechumens are dismissed after the liturgy of the word. They continue to share the word with a catechist in a suitable place.

Jim Dunning, in an unpublished lecture, gives several reasons why parishes should not dismiss the dismissal:

- It is an act of hospitality—you do not invite people to a meal in which they cannot partake.
- It is an invitation to savor the real presence of God in the word.
- It creates a hunger for the eucharist.

- The eucharist is then seen as the climax of initiation.
- The best catechetical time is in the context of worship in the midst of the community.
- The lectionary becomes the basic text for the journey.
- The dismissal is a challenge to Catholics to ask why they remain.
- It becomes an invitation to others in the community who are not yet initiated fully to come and see.

Many parishes are dismissing the catechumens and candidates. They use the time after dismissal as the basic catechetical session of the journey. In some places in North America, the catechumens and candidates come forward before the dismissal and are given a special blessing or are anointed with the oil of catechumens. This procedure certainly will vary according to local custom. It is important, however, that the dismissal be done with reverence and in full view of the assembly. Symbols can evangelize.

Pastorally, the dismissal seems to break down during the Three Days—the Easter Triduum. Do you dismiss the elect on Holy Thursday and Good Firday? The answer is yes. The problem is not with the logic of the dismissal, but with the practical problem of what you do for the catechist who goes with them since there is only one opportunity for communion on those days. Parishes need to work out this procedure, and perhaps allow the catechist to share in the eucharist after the catechetical session. In any case, do not dismiss the dismissal on Holy Thursday or Good Friday.

Another pastoral adaptation that needs challenging is the practice of receiving the candidates for full communion into the church on Holy Thursday during the evening celebration. This practice stems from the desire to allow these candidates to experience fully the celebrations of the first two days of the Triduum. This practice is questionable for two reasons. First, it confuses the candidates for full communion with penitents, who traditionally were brought back to the table of the Lord on Holy Thursday. With the redevelopment of the order of penitents, we need to clearly distinguish these two groups. The candidates are not penitents primarily. Second, the practice is a witness to a real misunderstanding of the rhythm of the Triduum. The Easter Vigil eucharist, not that of Holy Thursday, is the primary celebration of the Lord's death and resurrection. The celebration of initiation, in the case of the candidates by a profession of faith and confirmation, is climaxed at the Vigil by the sharing of the eucharist. On a personal level, it would seem unfair to the candidates themselves to bring them into full communion before the actual Paschal night, when the whole church is praying and fasting in anticipation of this celebration of initiation.

The Period of Mystagogia: Eastertime

At Sunday Masses throughout the Easter Season, the neophytes should keep their special places among the faithful. All the neophytes should take part in the Mass with their godparents. They should be mentioned in the homily and the general intercessions. (RCIA, #236)

With this rubric, a picture of the Easter season is sketched—a vision not always realized at the parish. As the scrutinies are the least celebrated of the rites, mystagogia is the least alive of the RCIA's periods. Besides being a period to celebrate and joyfully welcome the neophytes into the community, mystagogia leads the neophytes to the real significance of their initiation: Christian ministry for the life of the world. Perhaps mystagogia is the least alive of the seasons because it breaks down where most of our parishes do—in celebrating the call of the Lord in service beyond the parish boundaries. Keeping the mission orientation of the period in mind, how can a parish fittingly celebrate the Fifty Days?

Easter Sunday Eucharist and Easter Vespers

Special attention should be given to Easter Day. This includes special planning not only for the Masses of the day but also for evening prayer which concludes the Triduum. On Easter Sunday, the neophytes come to a designated eucharistic celebration. They enter the assembly during the opening procession. They wear their white garments and take a special place in the assembly—a place of honor. The neophytes may be invited to stand around the altar at the eucharistic prayer and communion.

It is highly recommended that the neophytes do not do any liturgical ministry (i.e., reader, communion minister, etc.) for an entire year. This will give them time to be involved in ministries of service before they serve the assembly at the eucharist. Nevertheless, their presence at the altar during the Sundays of Easter would certainly be a living icon of God's faithful love for us all.

Parish planners are highly encouraged to celebrate Easter Sunday vespers with the neophytes and the entire parish. Do not allow fatigue to decide—save some energy for this most prayerful close of the Triduum. Fine examples of this rite can be found in *A Triduum Sourcebook* (LTP, 1983) and *The Fifty Days* (Liturgical Conference, 1983). During vespers, the neophytes may again wear their white garments. The celebration traces the steps of the previous night and celebrates thankful praise to God for all the works of Christ.

The Eucharistic Celebration with the Diocesan Bishop

During the Easter season, along with the parish celebrations, the diocese gathers all the newly initiated for a eucharistic celebration with the bishop. This celebration, planned by those in the diocese who work with the catechumenate, should speak clearly of the joy of baptism and Christian service. Let all the symbols speak boldly. Every care is given to make this event significant for the whole diocese.

Some dioceses are celebrating these Masses outside of the cathedral in regional gatherings. This keeps the groups smaller and more personal for the bishop to address.

As mentioned earlier, a letter from the bishop inviting each neophyte to this celebration is highly recommended.

The Pentecost: The Fiftieth Day

The RCIA suggests that a parish celebration be held near Pentecost Sunday to close the period of mystagogy (RCIA, #237). In that same paragraph, a party is recommended. (An interesting rubric!) This might be linked with a party for those young people who are celebrating first eucharist or confirmation. The parish could have a celebration of all those initiated at any level of membership in the church. The springtime would certainly come alive.

The Pentecost eucharist, with its color and imagery, concludes the mystagogy period. A practice developing in North America is to invite the neophytes to give public testimony at the celebration. They would testify about the meaning of their experiences of conversion and initiation; they would share the form of ministry they will continue or begin as they go forward to renew the face of the earth.

"To do the best you can, Father, that's what saints are made of!" That phrase fits well as we conclude this whirlwind tour of the seasons of enlightenment and mystagogia. In all our planning of these rites of the RCIA, we must remember that we are making Christians—saints—who can do the best they can to transform the market place, the school, the home, the world into the reign of God. Do not lose heart.

Environment and Art

John Buscemi

CAUTION: If you are looking here for ten new and snappy decorating ideas for Lent and Eastertime, you will be disappointed. Worship spaces are like the people who gather within them. They come big and small; urban, suburban and rural; overdressed and sloppy, pretentious and down-home; old and young, aloof and welcoming, bright and dour—sometimes they are just right. It is impossible to find perfect, one-size-fits-all solutions for creating a conducive environment for worship.

This chapter challenges readers to scrutinize their own liturgical space. Three things are offered as helps in the looking: a general outlook, a description of common types of spaces, and some design concepts for Lent and Eastertime.

A General Outlook

"God does not need liturgy; people do, and people have only their own arts and styles of expression with which to celebrate." Oftentimes these words catch people off guard. Those most perplexed are the ones who sit in our liturgical assemblies with arms folded, eyes glazed and jaws resolutely set. They are the ones who endure "attending Mass" because they believe that somehow God is overjoyed by the magnanimity of their passive gesture. The bold statement above is from *Environment and Art in Catholic Worship*, prepared by the Bishops' Committee on the Liturgy in 1978. By taking the time to break open this statement and search its rich insight, the importance of liturgical art and environment can be focused and the task of the artist clarified. Two elements are packed together here and demand attention. The first is the overwhelmingly clear insistence that the liturgy must be oriented to people. The second element sets out the tools at our disposal.

God does not need liturgy; people do . . .

God is not robbed of praise nor denied worship when the liturgy of the church is people-centered and people-directed. Liturgical action which is sensitive to the cares and needs of the people helps us avoid the stinging judgment of the Hebrew Scriptures in which God's wrath is provoked by hollow rituals performed by absent-minded, empty-hearted participants. People-directed liturgy responds to the mandate of Jesus that the Sabbath observance sustain belief, rather than make people subservient to its rituals.

Many threads from scripture can be woven together to show that authentic praise of God, authentic worship, begins when the assembly gathers to remember. We, the assembly, gather to remember that we are a chosen and beloved people; to remember the mighty deeds of a liberating God; to remember the incarnate Word—Emmanuel, God-with-us; to remember that no one or nothing stands alone, and that everything is connected, related and joined into an intricate tapestry of unspeakable richness. This is our story.

In order to remember all this, as well as the brokenness in our community, the fractured state of our gathering, and our constant need for healing, the liturgy is the essential arena in which the story can be imaginatively told over and over. The liturgy must provide a vehicle for story telling and remembering of such power and clarity that we will never be tempted to forget. Forgetfulness is the root of sinfulness. To continuously tell the story is the sure safeguard against forgetfulness. The role of the liturgy is to help us remember and to celebrate the network of sustaining relationships with creation, within ourselves, with others and with God. All these levels of relationship must be cultivated through the liturgy.

When liturgy is seen as the arena for remembrance through story telling we can appreciate the profound ordinariness of the task before us. The whole human family delights in stories told with eagerness around campfires and kitchen tables, in living rooms and on journeys. Our stories celebrate great events, narrate history, ease sorrow, cause laughter, give instruction, speak to the heart, heal and lovingly nurture. Nathan Mitchell says: "People do not simply tell stories, they *live* in the stories they tell." Jesus knew this better than anyone. Through his stories and parables he crafted for us a home in which we can live and know love. More than this, Jesus made his whole life into an enacted parable: "The storyteller became the story."

To return again to the bishops' statement, we might be able to express its meaning more fully if we say: God does not need liturgy, because God does not forget the story and has been faithful to it. People, on the other hand, need liturgy because it is an essential mode of remembering and telling our story. Liturgy at its best rescues us from chronic amnesia.

People have only their own arts . . .

Important stories are always better told when all the arts can be employed in the effort. Life-giving, life-sustaining stories are never simple, journalistic just-the-facts-ma'am narratives. Stories in which we can live always have layer upon layer of meaning—they have many entrances and exits—all wrapped around a core insight.

In my mind's eye the best stories come in two varieties. One type is like marvelous Victorian houses with many rooms and in many shapes, on many floors. Houses of this style and vintage offer many vantage points, spaces and moods. Our faith story, in the same way, can be given a full range of expression through the arts. The second variety of story may be likened to a Japanese-style home in which a central room can accommodate a variety of needs and functions. This is a space where the economy of form, line, texture and color is highly prized. From this type of space flows the axiom of Mies van der Rohe: "Less is more and God is in the details." Here, the arts hone and focus the attention of the sensitive observer. Here the macrocosm is captured in the microcosm; mystery saturates the ordinary. The effect is much more in tune with abstract art than pictorial realism.

It would be wonderful if everyone had the luxury of having both kinds of spaces. The human psyche is able to travel back and forth between them easily. It needs both of them. However, while few of us have such variety in our living spaces, we can possess this range of richness for our story telling. This demands the careful cultivation of all the arts. Unfortunately, when the arts are poorly used, or excluded altogether, our story of salvation is truncated and impoverished. Our story resembles neither the self-confident exuberance of the Victorian style nor the profound simplicity of the Japanese style. Often our story telling is more like the boring ticky-tacky boxes which dot much of our landscape. Piled high, they serve as urban high rises; strung together, they form many a suburban tract—all are containers for people, not environments in which to *live* our story. The story we tell in the liturgy must be enriched and expressed through the arts if we are to avoid being trapped within anonymous and sterile boxes.

In summary, the introductory statement from *Environment and Art in Catholic Worship* weaves together two important principles. The first sets before us the idea that people-directed and people-centered liturgy provides the vehicle for the narration of our covenant story. Only through remembrance of our story can authentic worship be offered. The second principle supplies us with the tools for story telling—the arts. Their sensitive use provides both the range and the depth needed for significant story telling.

A New Aesthetic

A great deal of space has been devoted here to establishing these two principles. Undoubtedly, they will not be new for many readers. However, my experience has been that a gap exists between theory and practice; between the principles and the artistic forms which attempt to give them expression. These two principles can prompt a new aesthetic for liturgical spaces. Artists, then, will no longer be considered, or consider themselves, as mere decorators for the liturgical seasons as if their job is to add the fluff and frosting to word-laden ritual. The aesthetic task flowing from a liturgy for people and their story telling forces artists to offer their gifts as an authentic service which is necessary to the well-being of the community and to the story it tells. The task of the artist is not to decorate around a theme or a message in the fashion of medieval manuscript illuminators. The result, no matter how beautiful, was superfluous to the written word. Rather, artists must direct their talents towards creating environments in which the community can tell a truthful and complete story—towards creating an environment in which we can live our story. The task at its most basic level is to use the visual arts to help the assembly be better storytellers, better rememberers.

One more caution. A new aesthetic demands new solutions and new uses for the arts within our assemblies. New solutions demand a period of time during which judgment is suspended—a time for exploring which begins with actually seeing what is there.

Types of Worship Space

At first encounter every church presents to an observer a mood or an impression. Try to look at your worship space with fresh and critical eyes. Discover what it says to the first-time visitor. Generally, I observe four types of space.

The "Neo-" Church

The first type is those *pre*conciliar spaces which are neo-Gothic, neo-Romanesque or neo-Baroque in style. Here the eye can wander over a veritable encyclopedia of color, pattern and ecclesial imagery. Here, also, the emphasis is usually biased in favor of private, devotional practices rather than a *liturgical* emphasis upon the assembly, altar, ambo and baptismal font. When doing anything visual in these churches, take great care to bring the liturgical aspects of the room more clearly into focus. Often seasonal "decorating" only increases the visual clutter and further obscures the presence of ministers, altar, ambo and font. For instance, when the large banks of flowers often used at Christmas and Easter are massed in front of the altar, the result usually forces the altar to become the backdrop rather than the central visual reminder of our table-fellowship. It is better to leave that space unencumbered and to let the flowers speak their beauty from another spot.

Fifties-Sparse

Another type of space emerged in the 1950s and continued to develop through the conciliar years. These worship spaces are of utmost simplicity—spaces with an almost monastic quality. While they clearly have a liturgical emphasis, they often seem unable to give full visual expression to the range of human emotions needed to tell our whole story. At times these spaces are too restrained for parish life—appealing more to the head than the whole person. They cry out for color, pattern and texture. Over the years some of these spaces have become increasingly cluttered. This, of course, does violence to the architectural integrity of the room. Artists who work in this type of space must always remember that a little goes a long way. Making the space expressive is important, but an economy of expression is the key.

The Gym

Also evolving through the 1950s and the conciliar era were spaces destined to become the great gymnasiums and auditoriums of a vast school complex. On the way, however, they had to function for a few years as a church. Unfortunately for many parishes the few years have stretched out to decades. In the end these parishes got neither their gymnasiums nor their effective liturgical spaces. Minimal aesthetic considerations and a great emphasis upon practicality have severely compromised full liturgical expression. In the best of these places skilled artists have been able to turn the anonymity and flexibility of the room into a liturgical advantage. More often, however, these places do for liturgy what a black-and-white television does for the Rose Bowl Parade.

Contemporary Solutions

The fourth type of space is newer, postconciliar construction that seriously wrestles with the implications of a theology of assembly. These forms and spaces convincingly emphasize the gathered community as the primary liturgical symbol. They are, as yet, very embryonic. The solutions they set out are as tentative as they are exciting. Above all, these spaces endeavor to be hospitable environments in a human scale.

These spaces parallel the dynamic of our own homes in which the role of a gracious host or hostess is to create a place of welcome and acceptance, not a place that intimidates with its power or awes by its richness. Good hosts and hostesses use everything within the environment to help guests sense that they are valued and important. The environment helps to encourage communication and festivity. When people can be at ease and know that they are valued, then sharing, praise and story telling are enhanced. A central theme of *Environment and Art in Catholic Worship* is this: "Liturgy flourishes within a climate of hospitality." The new spaces attempt to give form to this theme through processional entrances, gathering areas, lighting, crafted details, color, texture, pattern, the arrangement of seating and the placement of areas for music, word, table and font. Hospitality for the Christian assembly is patterned on the hospitality we shower upon favored guests within our homes.

Assess Your Space

No matter which type of worship space is yours, begin to assess it according to the demands of hospitality. Artists who work in these spaces, make sure that all you do increases the hospitable feeling. Never allow your efforts to become art for art's sake, art for personal ego-gratification, or art which obstructs people-centeredness. Let the general and seasonal environments you create put people at ease because they know they are welcome. Put people in touch with each other rather than forcing them to read a banner or to figure out a cryptic message locked within a lenten or Easter display. The hospitable environment also demands that our efforts break out of the "sanctuary" space. Even though the communion rails may be long gone, the emphasis of much artistic effort says that there are really two separate spaces—one of them clearly more important than the other. This misguided emphasis reinforces clericalism and is lacking theological truth.

A new aesthetic involves the whole space of the community—from the parking lot to the table and out again. Robert Hovda describes this well when he likens a good liturgical celebration (and we might add a good worship environment) to the parables and stories of the gospels. Good celebration, he says, "puts us momentarily in the promised and challenging reign of God, where we are treated like we have never been treated anywhere else . . ., where we are bowed to and sprinkled and censed and kissed and touched and where we share equally among all a holy food and drink." Accomplishing this vision is a worthy task for any artist. It starts with creating a hospitable, human and humane environment. To give a name, then, to the artistic task and to the aesthetic we seek for our liturgical spaces is to name and then to use everything we know about hospitality.

Design Concepts

Ashes

Ash Wednesday, while not a day of obligation, has a power in people's lives. The ceremony of ashes draws large numbers of people. Ashes themselves and the signing with ashes are a strong visual statement. Often this power is ignored in favor of a host of other "lenten" images. A commonsense, but often violated, architectural axiom applies here: First, observe where people are walking, then design the placement of the sidewalks. Focus on the ashes.

Traditionally, ashes are made of dried palm branches saved from the previous year. If this is your custom, save enough to make a bundle of them to be displayed for the people to see—perhaps at the entrances of the church. Also, consider having the sign of ashes present throught Lent as a way for people to recall the words: "Repent and believe in the Good News." Beautiful ceramic bowls would work well as containers.

A Visual Fast

The feasts of Christmas, Easter and Pentecost are the three main chapters of our story. Lent is *a time of preparation* for catechumens and for the community. It is the passageway to Easter, but often it has been made an end in itself. This proves once again that Catholics are much more comfortable with themes like sin, guilt, hell-fire and brimstone, rather than with festival and celebration. Let the environment of Lent continue to let Christians know that, although we are in need of healing, we are indeed saved. While flawed, we are indeed loved. The atmosphere for worship should call us to both introspection and communal growth, but it should never lack in the basics of hospitality and good fellowship. I believe a certain starkness is called for during this season. It is a time of visual fasting, so to speak, in preparation for the feasting of Easter. This is contrary to those who insist on adding more and more visual elements during Lent—a sort of "visual snacking." For me, visual fasting means stripping away all but the essentials. Even those things should be as simple as possible. Wasn't visual fasting the intention behind covering the statues during Passiontide? Maybe the task is to perform some visual editing of the worship space rather than adding anything during this season.

Create a Mood

Beware of visual images and objects selected for their message potential. The key is to create a mood, not to be cerebral. Words like "Lent," "pray," "fast," "almsgiving," "grow," "hope," "repent," etc. do not accomplish what they state, anymore than words like "celebrate" and "rejoice" can ensure a festival. Using words as decoration is a distracting visual pollution. Mood is created by subtler things like color and lighting and arrangements of natural objects such as twigs and stones.

A mood is also created by empty spaces. A suitable lenten atmosphere is one in which people know that they have come to a place of searching rather than to a place of cliches and easy solutions. The mood, the place I seek during Lent is described by Paul Goldberger, the architectural critic of the *New York Times*:

> It is a room of beautiful serenity, yet one of movement and action at the same time. It pulls us forward, it holds us back. It holds us tight, it lets us go. It joins us together, it holds us apart. It ultimately tells us that for all we know, there is something we do *not* know, something that we will never be able to fully understand.

A space which can do this is also a space where opposites can be reconciled and a sense of wholeness can be experienced.

The Triduum Symbols

The symbols through which we tell our story are nowhere more intensely and clearly clustered than in the Triduum. They are to the Christian story what color, pattern and form are to the artist. The symbols presented in the Triduum are assembly, cross, oil, water, word, light, bread, wine, laying on of hands, and foot washing. However, we must go further than this list, because our symbols are more than things; they contain actions. Therefore, we can say that our symbols include the assembly, but it is the assembly gathered for praise and thanksgiving, the cross that is signed, oil for anointing, water flowing and giving life, light that is passed to all, bread broken and wine shared, the laying on of hands as actual touching, foot washing expressed as intercessory prayer and works of service. In the liturgy the sacred is mediated through these active symbols. Aidan Kavanagh says it best:

> When the Easter Vigil "speaks" about initiation, it does so in terms that are a veritable evangelization of the cosmos. Fire, water, wax, bees, light and darkness, bread, wine, aromas, tough and graceful words and gestures — all these stand as a context without which what happens to one entering corporate faith in Jesus Christ is only partially perceptible.

When we realize the impact of our symbols as "evangelization of the cosmos," when we can unleash their visual and artistic power, then it becomes obvious how trivial and second-rate many of our Eastertime decorating schemes really are. Level upon level of lilies in foil-wrapped and bow-bedecked pots, swag-draped crosses, papier-mache butterflies with ten-foot wing spans and spring gardens meandering through sanctuary spaces will never have the power of our primary, liturgical symbols. We need to use all the artistic skills available to us so that the symbols of the Triduum can permeate the whole Easter season. Do nothing which obscures, competes with, or compromises them.

Can You See The Feast?

A sense of balance and flow are important to the liturgical year. Have you ever put in so much work for the preparation of a party that you were too tired to enjoy it? I've noticed, especially in liturgy committees, a great sigh of relief when Easter arrives. The Vigil signifies more that Lent is over than the entrance into the festival. Balance and flow are important. What happens when the lilies die? Does that signify the end of the Easter season more than the celebration of Pentecost? In rethinking the environments for worship maybe we must also rethink the seasons upon which we place our greatest emphasis. Maybe the lenten emphasis should diminish so that the Easter-to-Pentecost cycle can be the context for the myriad springtime events that occupy our assembly. If Lent is visual fasting, make sure that Eastertime provides a true season of feasting—both inside and outside the worship space.

Artists, no matter what the season, you honor the Christian assembly and live up to the grace of your ministry if you can help create an environment in which people are nurtured. The people of God are fed by the visual arts. Through the arts the members of the assembly can experience the place in which they gather as one which reveres creation, helps to share burdens through signs of welcome, and, finally, calls the assembly to praise God with thanksgiving.

Music

JoAnne Timmerman

The mystery of our faith is never more penetrating than during the seasons of Lent and Eastertime. The liturgy planning must spring from the Triduum as the fulcrum which draws us into the fasting and the feasting. We also take our lead from the *Rite of Christian Initiation of Adults*. These days are not a time to remember the historical events of Jesus' life. It is not a time to wish away our sins, rather, it is an honest attempt to face again our need for conversion. Music is a vehicle which carries us on this journey. It catches our inner self and conveys the conversion of the heart when our words fall short. We sing of mercy, forgiveness, a change of heart, a desert, a mountain experience, of seeing, washing and rising. Eastertime proclaims alleluias, glorias, gatherings, sendings and spirit.

The key aid to entering into this process is familiarity with the tools of worship. The assembly needs to know what is expected; people can pray best with music they know. The two seasons have parallel planning details. During Lent we can emphasize the penitential rite and in Eastertime replace it with the rite of sprinkling to celebrate our baptism. If the lenten acclamations are in a minor key or mode, use the major key in Eastertime. A common responsorial psalm asking for mercy gives way to a psalm of rejoicing and gladness for Easter. Now let us look more closely to some possibilities for this season.

Ash Wednesday

The ashes are usually blessed and distributed between the liturgy of the word and the liturgy of the eucharist on Ash Wednesday; however, the blessing and giving of ashes may be done in a word service. According to the sacramentary, the liturgy of the word provides the structure for this: entrance song, opening prayer, readings with a responsorial psalm, homily, blessing and distribution of ashes, general intercessions. Another context for the signing with ashes may be the liturgy of the hours—morning prayer or vespers. The structure of this liturgy would be: call to prayer, hymn, psalms, readings, homily, distribution of ashes, canticle, litany of prayers, the Lord's Prayer, concluding prayer.

In any structure, this entrance into the lenten journey sets the tenor for all the liturgies to come. Some opening hymns may include "Hosea's Song" (Weston Priory), "Save Us, O Lord" by Bob Dufford, (NALR). "Out of the Depths" by Marty Haugen (GIA) or a more traditional hymn such as those found in *Worship II* (which lists the hymns in a liturgical index according to feast and season), the *Catholic Book of Worship* from the Canadian Catholic Conference and the new edition of *Peoples Mass Book* from World Library Publications. A suggested hymn from the latter is "This Is Our Accepted Time." In any liturgy the purpose of the opening hymn is to unify and set the direction of that particular gathering. If there is a procession, the hymn sung by the assembly gathers our hearts and minds as the scene takes shape. The opening hymn should be familiar so that all may enter this lenten journey firmly. If the distribution of ashes is during a liturgy of the word, the ashes and the word are the focus. Remove whatever calls attention to the altar. Lighting, environment and placement focus attention on the ambo and ashes.

The responsorial psalm belongs to the assembly. It is their response to the call to repentance heard in the reading from Joel. This would be the key time to introduce a common response to be used throughout Lent. Many composers and publishing companies are providing simple, yet interesting psalm refrains. Among them are: *Psalms for Feasts and Seasons* by Christopher Willcock (PAA), *Celebrating Liturgy, Accompaniment for Seasonal Responsorial Psalms* (LTP), the *Gelineau Gradual* (the antiphons are given in *Worship II*, GIA), and *Psalms for the Church Year* by Marty Haugen and David Haas (GIA). The great advantage of the common response is that the assembly is freer to pray the response instead of concentrating on learning even the shortest response in one hearing. This refrain can serve as a "theme song" rising out of the heart during the week, bringing to mind the journey of these days. A disadvantage may be that after a couple of Sundays, the common response can become lifeless and generate a lack of interest. If this is the case, a second response may be introduced; the two can be interchanged during the Sundays of Lent. There may be some parishes or assemblies of worship, such as novitiates, priories or hospitals where the response of the day would be preferred.

The *Gelineau Gradual* which uses the antiphons in *Worship II* and the new *Peoples Mass Book* have various psalm responses. Other psalm settings are available from sources for morning prayer: *Praise God in Song* (GIA) and *Morning Praise and Evensong* (Fides Publishers). During the distribution of ashes various hymns and psalms may be sung. Since this is a procession, an antiphonal style piece is preferred to aid the assembly in singing.

The beginning of the season is an appropriate time to introduce the singing of the general intercessions. The cantor prays the short intercessory prayers inviting the assembly to respond with "Lord hear our prayer." The Ash Wednesday music will introduce the journey into Lent, and set the style and manner of worship during the days of repentance.

Sundays of Lent

Cycle A

The lectionary for cycle A is most attuned to the rites of Christian initiation. If these rites are celebrated within the Sunday liturgies, the A cycle readings may be substituted during cycles B and C. The first readings throughout the six Sundays trace the call of God's people: a people created out of love (Gen 2), called to minister God's blessing to the nations (Gen 12), sometimes doubting (Ex 17), a chosen race (1 Sam 16), a pilgrim people enlivened by the Spirit of the Lord God (Ez 37). The theology of St. Paul as seen in the letters to the Romans, 2 Timothy and Ephesians emphasizes our baptismal faith. The temptations in the desert and the transfiguration on the mountain are common to all three cycles for the first and second Sundays of Lent, however, in the A cycle, the gospel develops the focus on conversion with the stories of the woman of Samaria, the man born blind and the raising of Lazarus. North American Liturgy Resources has published *Path of Life* by the Dameans specifically for the rites of the RCIA. Besides being used as hymns and acclamations with the initiation rites, these songs can be repeated during other parts of the liturgy to unify and emphasize the journey of conversion for all the faithful. For example, the fourth Sunday's reading from Romans reads: "Awake, O Sleeper, and rise from the dead." The gospel speaks of the man born blind, coming from darkness to the light of faith. "Awake, O Sleeper" could be the entrance hymn to unify our voices and thrust us into this liturgy. In *Gather to Remember* (GIA) Marty Haugen's "Show Us the Path of Life" is another version of Psalm 16 useful for the RCIA or journey theme. From this same source is a setting of Psalm 62–63, "Your Love Is Finer Than Life," a possibility for a common psalm response or antiphonal communion song. Though it is an "Advent" hymn, "Awake, Awake, Fling Off the Night," from the *Catholic Book of Worship* uses the same lyrics, and may be suitable. Other hymns for the RCIA can be found in the liturgical index for seasons and feasts in *Worship II*. *Peoples Mass Book* has a section on the *Rite of Christian Initiation of Adults* which includes psalms and hymns.

Cycle B

The notions of commandment and covenant pervade the first readings of the B cycle. In Genesis, Noah receives the promise of God's fidelity; Abraham is presented as our father in faith; Moses meets God on the mountain to bring the commandments to the people. In 2 Chronicles, we hear the infidelities of this chosen nation and in Jeremiah, the promise of a new covenant.

The second readings bring out the difficulties of being faithful and the stumbling block of the cross against the mercy of a forgiving God. The gospels of the third, fourth and fifth Sundays from John lay before us the theme of death and rising to new life. "My Song Is Love Unknown" (*Worship II*) has beautiful four-part harmonies; in a traditional style this hymn captures the Johannine focus of surrendering one's life to the will of the Father. As a choral hymn during the preparation of the gifts it would allow the assembly to concentrate on the message of the gospel. In *Glory and Praise*, vol. 3 (NALR), two hymns carry this theme: "Only This I Want" by Dan Schutte and "We Were Strangers" by Lucien Deiss. The text of "If God Is for Us" is taken directly from the readings of this cycle.

Cycle C

As in cycle B the first, second and sixth Sundays tell the same gospel stories but this time from Luke. The gospels of the third, fourth and fifth Sundays make reconciliation a focus of this series of readings. The first readings trace the development of the relationship of our ancestors in faith: Moses, Abram, Joshua and Isaiah; the Lord God calls and sustains Israel in life and in faith. The second readings from Paul exhort us to remain faithful. As examples to the elect, we all witness to the process of conversion, i.e., the race Paul talks of in Philippians. The call of reconciliation is most clear in the story of the prodigal son (fourth Sunday) and the woman caught in adultery John (fifth Sunday). Not only is conversion demanded from the characters of these stories but the conversion of the bystanders is the hidden plot.

Some music for this series might be: "Yahweh the Faithful One," "Only This I Want" (NALR); antiphons and/or hymns taken from Psalms 22, 51, 63 and 130, see *Peoples Mass Book* for "O God, My God" (#188), "Have Mercy, Lord, on Us" (#196), "O God, You Are My God" (#198), "Lord, from the Depths I Cry to You" (#213); also "Forgive Our Sins as We Forgive" (#276) and "From the Depths of Sin and Sadness" (#279) from *Catholic Book of Worship*. There are beautiful choral editions of lenten hymns, such as "Were You There" (for Holy Week) and "Amazing Grace" that could be used as meditation pieces before the liturgy or at the preparation of the gifts.

Except for suggestions that refer to the responsorial psalms, the hymns listed above are best used during processions or after communion when a hymn may be used to gather as one in thanksgiving and praise. Ideally the people will be familiar with the hymn, and the choir will be free to add descants and four-part harmony.

Palm Sunday

In all three cycles, Palm Sunday centers on the liturgy of the word. The blessing and distribution of palms and the gospel reading lead to a triumphant procession and the liturgies of the word and table. The major musical problem is the procession from an outside blessing place into the sanctuary. Taizé's "Jubilate, Servite," (*Music From Taizé,* GIA) in canon form can hold a procession together as much as possible. When most of the assembly have gathered in procession, the choir can help to hold together the singing. Another possible entrance hymn is "Let the King of Glory Come" by Michael Joncas (*On Eagle's Wings*, NALR); note that verses 2 and 3 are an Advent text and that verse 1 can be sung in call/response style. From *Worship II*, we have "Lift Up Your Heads, Ye Mighty Gates."

Sundays of Eastertime

Cycle A

After the great three days of the Triduum, the church continues to welcome the newly initiated. The mystogogia embraces these new Catholics, teaching them the ways of ministering and gathering. The readings from the Acts of the Apostles proclaim the words and works of the early church. We hear the words of Peter affirming and encouraging the church to witness and to proclaim the message of the resurrection. They met together and had all things in common. With the exception of the Emmaus story from Luke, the gospels during this time are from John. The scene of these resurrection stories is the upper room, the place of the first eucharist.

The development of the assembling church permeates the Sundays of Easter. The hymns of these liturgies are filled with alleluia and praise. One voice, one body, one church proclaims the hope of resurrection. Many of the traditional hymns work well to gather and unify us for celebration: "Jesus Christ Is Risen Today," "Hail Thee, Festival Day," "Christ the Lord Is Risen Today," "On This Day the First of Days," "The Strife Is O'er, the Battle Done" from *Worship II*; "Let the Earth Rejoice and Sing," "This Is the Day" (also a suitable common responsorial psalm throughout Easter-time) from *Peoples Mass Book*. More contemporary hymns are: "City of God," "Awake O Sleeper," "Lift Up Your Hearts," "Let the Earth Resound," "In Those Days," and others from *Glory & Praise*, vol. 3. (NALR); "Canticle of the Sun," "He Is the Lord," "Praise Canticle," "Praise the Lord, My Soul," and as a common response, "Let All the Earth," all from *Gather to Remember* (GIA).

Cycle B

The consistent element of this series is the second reading from the First Letter of John. There is a resting in the knowledge that we are truly loved by God; the joy of the Easter season dominates. The first reading from the Acts of the Apostles speaks of the developing Christian community. The gospel (the first three Sundays are the same as cycle A) takes us from the resurrection to the theme of the Good Shepherd to "missioning" with the Spirit. Many of the same hymns listed for cycle A would work here as well. Some hymns more specific to these readings are: "The Lord Is My Shepherd" or "The Lord Is My True Shepherd," "I Am the Vine," *Peoples Mass Book*.

Cycle C

The gospels during this cycle are not unlike the gospels of the other two cycles. Added elements are the fishing story, the shepherd theme, the call for unity and the promise of the Spirit. Though the first reading is from the Acts of the Apostles, the focus is different: the persecution of the early church. The Book of Revelation encourages the listener, urging fidelity to the Lord. The uniqueness of this cycle is the consequence of our commitment to the Lord, i.e., persecution and the hope of a new Jerusalem. Some hymns that deal with this theme are: "O Holy City, Seen of John," "Rejoice, the Lord Is King," "Heavenly Host in Ceaseless Worship" and Psalm 92, "The Lord Is King" from *Worship II*. In *Praise God in Song* (GIA), there are canticles from the Book of Revelation that may be used as responsorial psalms and/or antiphonal processional hymns.

Service Music for Lent

All that has been said to this point refers to hymns that are variable and seasonal. Their purpose is to emphasize the season and to unify those assembled so that they become receptive to hear the word of God and respond in thanksgiving. If the entire assembly is to celebrate, they need to be familiar with the elements of worship. Though the music director may be constantly tempted to have new and exciting hymns, the liturgy is for the people, not the people for the liturgy. How can we make the familiar interesting and inviting and introduce new elements gradually? In *Worship II* and *Peoples Mass Book* some of the classic hymns have contemporary lyrics. A choir can add harmonies to selected verses. Asking the assembly to alternate sides or asking men to alternate with the women, can be a challenge to the assembly. Instruments such as timpani and/or brass can brighten an old hymn.

Now we turn to those musical elements of the liturgy which are not variable; service music refers to those parts of the liturgy, i.e., litanies, the responsorial psalm and acclamations. The flavor of the service music during Lent ought to be different from that of Eastertime. Lent is an opportune time to develop the penitential rite. There are many musical contributions to enhance this litany: some led by the cantor with the assembly repeating the "Lord, have mercy," others led by the choir with the repeated phrase in harmony with the assembly. A publication from NALR called *Shout For Joy!* contains service music for keyboard and/or guitar accompaniment from various composers. Another possibility for the penitential rite is to introduce to the assembly a motif or constantly repeated pattern with the text "Lord, have mercy." Over that mantra-style phrase, the cantor chants the call for mercy. Since the Gloria is not sung during Lent, a sung penitential rite can give proper balance and flow to the introductory rites.

Having been prepared to hear the word of God, we listen and then respond. The responsorial psalm captures that response for us with the universal response of the psalter. Most commonly, the antiphon is first sung by the cantor and repeated by the assembly; the cantor then sings the verses. If a different response is used each Sunday, it may be most clearly introduced by one person as cantor with the choir supporting the assembly in the response. Harmony may be added as the antiphon is repeated. As suggested earlier, the flavor of any liturgical season is emphasized when a common psalm response is used; the lectionary offers common texts for sung responsorial psalms. *Psalms for Feasts and Seasons* by Willcock, the *Gelineau Gradual* (GIA), and most participation aids provide a variety of common responses that can be used throughout the season. Since the major intention is to provide a most prayerful response, the less the assembly is taxed to learn something new, the more a prayerful atmosphere can be maintained.

The gospel acclamation is not simply tacked on to the second reading; rather, it is a call to rise and prepare our whole selves to hear the word of the gospel. Usually, there is movement during this time: the lector returns to the chair, the presider approaches the ambo and prepares to proclaim the gospel. The singing of the acclamation and this action ought to be evenly timed, so that when the acclamation is still resounding the presider extends his hands and declares, "The Lord be with you." Unlike the introduction to the hymn, the introduction to the acclamation is very short: one note on the keyboard or one chord from the guitar. The cantor or choir sings the acclamation first, then it is repeated by the assembly. If there is a verse, it is sung by the cantor/choir and again all repeat the acclamation with full voice.

After the homily or the rites of Christian initiation we have the general intercessions. Lent is an opportune time to sing these prayers, perhaps with the same response used during the penitential rite. To petition for mercy is to ask the Lord's continued and constant protection, that gratuitous love promised in the covenant. Repeating the petition can be a unifying factor, a frame for the liturgy of the word. Singing the intercessions flows best if the cantor sings simple and short petitions and indicates to the assembly when to respond. A choir can solidify that response and add harmony. A very familiar melody is the Byzantine chant as found in *Peoples Mass Book,* #580. There are other adaptations not only in that resource but also in *Shout for Joy!* (NALR: "Heavenly Father, Hear Us" by Joe Zsigray and "Litany" by Grayson W. Brown). Simplicity is the key; the petitions must be clear and short.

The preparation of the altar and gifts is very low-key. With the prayers of the faithful the liturgy of the word is closed and the liturgy of the eucharist begins. The preparation rite is simply the transition for this. There is always room for silence or for instrumental music. Allow the assembly time to internalize all that has been proclaimed in the readings and homily. Not only is the altar prepared, but the people need to prepare themselves to enter into the eucharist. The instrumental music may be a keyboard piece from the classical tradition or a familiar hymn played by flute or other solo intrument with instrumental accompaniment. Take care not to choose music that smacks of sweet Romanticism or feeds a "Jesus and me" syndrome. The choir may sing a choral piece that continues the seasonal theme. Ideally the length of the music should match the length of the ritual action.

The eucharistic acclamations are the Holy, the memorial acclamation and the Amen. In order for them to be sung as true acclamations they must have brief introductions and be familiar to the assembly. Be attentive to full settings of the eucharistic acclamations written by the same composer. For example, in *Peoples Mass Book* there is a Holy, memorial acclamation and Amen written by Jim Marchionda, all under the title *"Mass of Saint Dominic."* Similarly, in *Worship II* there are Masses by Richard Proulx, Alexander Peloquin and Howard Hughes; each of these compositions repeats musical patterns which help the singing of the acclamations. In *Shout For Joy!* Michael Joncas has two settings for the acclamation series; Bub Dufford has a familiar Holy with a Doxology and Amen. *Gather to Remember* from GIA is another source. It is not "mandatory" to sing acclamations that are written in a minor key during Lent, but modes and minor tones lend themselves to the flavor of the season.

It is often thought that to sing the Lord's Prayer excludes some of the assembly. However, there are simple settings that can be taught and sung. There are settings of the Lord's Prayer in *Peoples Mass Book*, *Worship II*, *Catholic Book of Worship* and *Shout For Joy!* With the Lord's Prayer we enter the communion rite. In the rhythm of the liturgy, this is another time of preparation. The body and blood of the Lord are prepared to be distributed to the faithful. The Lamb of God recalls our desire for mercy and peace. The litany needs to be extended to cover the preparation of plates and cups. There are contemporary versions of this litany in *Shout For Joy!*

and *Gather To Remember*. In *Peoples Mass Book* (#644) Eugene Englert has a litany in which the cantor/choir sings the petitions as the assembly responds with the refrain.

Service Music for Eastertime

All liturgical celebrations are centered around the great feast of the Triduum. From Ash Wednesday through Palm Sunday we prepare for an ever deepening journey into conversion. Once again we recall that we are the creatures, not the creator, and are in need of reconciliation. The great Three Days is the climax of this journey. Easter Sunday and the Fifty Days of Easter are the living out of that feast. The joy and intensity of Eastertime can be exhausting to sustain. But, the joy of Easter is to be a lasting peace. Alleluias now replace the repentance themes. The elements of the liturgy do not change, rather they indicate our conversion. No longer do we kneel and plead for mercy; the penitential rite would be well replaced with the water rite. If the font is movable it may be placed at the entrance of the church or in the center of the assembly. Begin the liturgy with the blessing of the water and the sprinkling rite. That is how we have all entered the church, as have the neophytes, with the water of baptism. If this is impossible, carry the bowl of water in the entrance procession, bless the water and proceed with the rite of sprinkling. Some appropriate hymns are "I Saw the Living Water" by Lucien Deiss, "You Will Draw Water" by Tom Conry, "The Goodness of God" by Gregory Norbet from *Glory and Praise*, vol. II (NALR); "O Healing River," a traditional Baptist hymn arranged by Michael Joncas in *Gather to Remember* (GIA). In *Peoples Mass Book* there are antiphons specifically for the rite of blessing and sprinkling holy water at Mass, #237 and #238.

Perhaps the Gloria could be sung during the sprinkling. Another way not to "overload" the introductory rite is to sing the Glory to God as the entrance hymn. Two other hymns that could be used as hymns of praise are from the monks of Taizé: "Gloria III" and "Jubilate, Servite" are two examples of canons (see *Gather to Remember* or *Music from Taizé* from GIA). Those settings that have a repeated antiphon include the assembly more easily in the singing of this hymn of praise.

What has been said for the responsorial psalm above holds true for Eastertime as well as Lent. The general response to the word of God heard on each particular Sunday is "Alleluia." Common responses are given in the lectionary as are many psalm suggestions in the hymnals. Some ideas: "Let All the Earth" by Marty Haugen and "This is the Day" in *Gather To Remember* (GIA); Willcock's *Psalms For Feasts and Seasons*, Haugen's and Haas' *Psalms for the Church Year* (GIA). The Damean's hymn "Alleluia" can be used as a common response and the refrain repeated for the gospel acclamation.

On the major feasts of Easter Day and Pentecost there is traditionally a sequence preceding the gospel. The purpose of this hymn is to prepare the listeners and to emphasize the gospel. Just as antiphons and familiar songs aid in reminding us of the words and work of God, so the intention is that the central words of the gospel sung in the sequence will help us to remember the events of this particular feast. However, pastorally it is questionable whether this purpose is really achieved. The musical style of the hymn may be uninviting to the contemporary ear. The assembly may become impatient with what seems to them an interruption of the liturgy. Therefore, the sequence needs to be evaluated from liturgical and pastoral points of view. Perhaps the sequence is better used as prelude, or after the gospel and homily as a "hymn of the day." Some possible musical settings for this hymn are: "Victimae Paschali," #290 in *Worship II*; in *Peoples Mass Book,* #384 in Latin and English, also #64, "Christ, the Lord, Is Ris'n Today." There seem to be more options for the Pentecost sequence: *Worship II,* #65, 62, 205; *Peoples Mass Book,* #403 (mode I chant), #87, 90, 92. The Taizé community has a canon based on "Veni Sancte Spiritus" which includes a cantor solo over a continuous motif (GIA).

Eastertime presents us with great reasons to proclaim the gospel greatly. Accentuate that proclamation with a procession to the ambo. During the procession the alleluia is sung. One example of an acclamation is: "Alleluia! Your Words" by Michael Joncas found in *Shout For Joy!* (NALR). In that same resource, there are other glorious settings of the alleluia. To cap off this climactic reading, repeat the alleluia after the reading. In order to lead into this recapitulation, ask the presider or deacon to sing the versicle "This is the gospel of the Lord." Then, giving only the first note or chord, acclaim the gospel with the alleluia again. This builds a sense of a feast day ritual. To do this every Sunday in Eastertime may be too much. This procedure gives emphasis to Easter and Pentecost, especially if the sequence has been sung.

After the homily and the creed, the general intercessions are introduced by the presider. As stated above, the singing of these prayers emphasizes this season. After listening during the homily, speaking the creed and singing the general intercessions, the preparation of the gifts should be low-key. What was stated earlier about silence and instrumental music during this time still holds true. This instrumental music can have a joyous flavor. A brass quartet or organ with trumpet would be bright and uplifting. This may be the time for the choir to sing an Easter motet or choral hymn, but it is important that the flow of the liturgy is not interrupted or delayed.

If ever eucharistic acclamations were to be "shouts of joy," it is now! A moving tempo, bright instruments, familiar music with harmonies make acclamations sound as they ought. Some composers have continuous acclamations similar to those used in the eucharistic prayers for children. In *Peoples Mass Book*, Donald J. Reagan has "Acclamations for Children's Eucharistic Prayer I," #599. Theophane Hytrek used eucharistic prayer II (#600) for a composition of acclamations. In *Shout For Joy!* Carey Landry has eucharistic acclamations arranged with a continuous keyboard accompaniment by Paul Page. In this same resource, Grayson W. Brown has a "Preface Dialogue" which would lead into the Holy. These continuous acclamations foster a communal sense of the flow of the prayer and give the assembly a greater sense of participation.

During Lent, the petitions of the Lamb of God ask for mercy and peace, but during Eastertime, direct the litany to the breaking of the bread. Ekklesia from Denver, Colorado, has a hymn for the breaking of bread which takes its text from the Emmaus story: "Breaking of the Bread" by Dan Feiten. In *Shout For Joy!* Tom Conry has two settings for this rite: "A Song for Breaking Bread" and "Fraction Rite: This Bread." This litany is not of high priority in the liturgy; yet, it does aid the flow of the communion rite and promote a sense of unity and receptivity for the eucharist. The hymn or antiphon during the communion procession is seasonal and continues to unify the assembly in their praise of the risen

Christ. After all have received communion a hymn of praise may be sung. Robert Edward Smith has an appropriate choral setting of the "Te Deum" using a repeated antiphon, with cantors or choir (GIA).

Consider supporting and encouraging the liturgy of the hours during the Lent and Easter seasons. This is a perfect time to return to the people this form of praying which was originally theirs. Liturgy Training Publications, Notre Dame and GIA have adapted this form for parish use. In the new edition of the *Peoples Mass Book*, #749 Morningsong and #755 Evensong provide hymns, psalms, canticles, for parish use. *Shout For Joy!* has variations of the Canticle of Mary. This prayer of the church returns to the people an ancient style of prayer that is rooted in scripture, tradition and history.

Bibliography of Music Resources

Biblical Hymns and Psalms, Lucien Deiss. World Library Publications, Inc., 3759 Willow Rd., Schiller Park IL 60176.

"Breaking of the Bread (The Road to Emmaus)," Dan Feiten. Ekklesia Music, Inc., 3750 South Hillcrest Dr., Denver CO 80237.

Catholic Book of Worship. Gordon V. Thompson Limited, 29 Birsh Ave., Toronto, Ontario M4V 1E2, and Publications Service, Canadian Catholic Conference, 90 Parent Ave., Ottawa, Ontario K1N 7B1.

Celebrating Liturgy: Accompaniment for Seasonal Responsorial Psalms. Liturgy Training Publications, 1800 North Hermitage Ave., Chicago IL 60622–1101.

Gather To Remember: Songs, Seasonal Psalms, Service Music, ed. by Michael A. Cymbala. G.I.A. Publications, Inc., 7404 South Mason Ave., Chicago IL 60638.

The Gelineau Gradual, Responsorial Psalms from the Lectionary for Mass for the Sundays and Principal Feasts of the Liturgical Year. G.I.A. Publications, Inc., 7404 South Mason Ave., Chicago IL 60638.

Glory and Praise: Songs for Christian Assembly, vols. I, II, III. North American Liturgy Resources, a division of Epoch Universal Publications, Inc., 10802 North 23rd Ave., Phoenix AZ 85029.

Lutheran Book of Worship. Augsburg Publishing House, 426 South 5th St., Minneapolis MN 55415.

Morning Praise and Evensong: A Liturgy of the Hours in Musical Setting, ed. and arranged by William G. Storey, Frank C. Quinn, OP, David F. Wright, OP, Fides Publishers, Inc., Notre Dame IN. [out of print]

Music from Taizé, vols. 1 and 2, Jacques Berthier. G.I.A. Publications, Inc., 7404 South Mason Ave., Chicago IL 60638.

Path of Life, Dameans. North American Liturgy Resources, Epoch Universal Publications, Inc., 10802 North 23rd Ave., Phoenix AZ 85029.

Peoples Mass Book, ed. Nicholas T. Freund, Getty Zins Reiber, Jeanne H. Schmidt. World Library Publications, Inc., 3759 Willow Rd., Schiller Park IL 60176.

Praise God in Song, ed. John Allyn Melloh, SM, and William G. Storey. G.I.A. Publications, Inc., 7404 South Mason Ave., Chicago IL 60638.

Psalms for the Church Year, Marty Haugen and David Haas. G.I.A. Publications, Inc., 7404 South Mason Ave., Chicago IL 60638.

Psalms for Feasts and Seasons: Settings of the Common Responsorial Psalms, Christopher Willcock, SJ. Pastoral Arts Associates of North America, Old Hickory TN 37138.

Shout For Joy! North American Liturgy Resources, Epoch Universal Publications, Inc., 10802 North 23rd Ave., Phoenix AZ 85029.

Worship II. G.I.A. Publications, Inc., 7404 South Mason Ave., Chicago IL 60638.

Preaching the Sundays of Lent and Eastertime

Ray Kemp

While preparing to write this piece, I came across an all too accepted line that states what I believe we ought to move *from*: "The goal of Lent is Easter." It is my experienced observation that Easter is not just the climax, but the end of this liturgical cycle in the practice of most of our parishes.

I want to share a different approach based on what has been learned from the *Rite of Christian Initiation of Adults* in Saint Augustine's Parish in Washington, DC. The growing conviction among parish ministers across the country who care about the initiation of adults substantiates the claim. Yes, the goal of Lent is Easter, but the goal of Lent and Eastertime is Pentecost—not so much Pentecost as a liturgical day, but as an event. Enlightenment/purification moves to Easter initiation, certainly, *and* Easter initiation moves through Easter reflection to a climax of celebrating who we are as church. Initiation is *for* something. That something is mission and ministry in a world the Lord would like us to re-create.

As a journeyer with elect and neophytes, I propose to examine this in three ways for preachers. First, we can see the 90 days of Lent and Easter as a "short course" in Catholic Christianity that ends in Pentecost. Second, we will experience a hint of the lectionary and prayers of Lent and Easter to taste the church as a community bent on conversion. Third, we will reflect on the goal of conversion and deliverance: the Spirit sending us into a world to re-create the face of the earth.

Our preaching is always done in a Catholic context as well as in a particular situation. The lectionary we share and the mysteries we celebrate make us one wherever we are. The unique demands and opportunities for your parish guide and control your making word and sacrament a real presence of the Christ in your corner of creation.

The Big 90: A Communal Passover

Forty days of Lent, 50 days of Easter, each with their own readings and prayers, are the heart of the life of the church. From the First Sunday of Lent when the church elects catechumens to Easter initiation, the faithful are called to lead them by prayer, fasting and good works and so experience their own reinitiation into Christ. Then, during Eastertime, the faithful with their neophytes are helped to realize just where Christ's saving power touched us, our families, our loves, indeed, our whole community of believers. Through this prayerful and festive consideration we are on a resolute pilgrimage to a renewed celebration of the sending of this parish into our world. Attend, all who would preach this season!

It is a world marching to a different drummer, preoccupied with success, safety and security. The big-timers concoct schemes for gaining more and the little folks struggle for survival. In spite of occasional and heroic evidence to the contrary, it is still a world that systematically shuns widows, orphans and aliens, cannot stomach prophets, jails and otherwise hunts down the ones who live the beatitudes. To be sure, a few committed ones receive the plaudits of the world, but recipients of peace prizes are ambushed and monetary awards to the Mother Teresas are soon spent with little noticeable effect on the human struggle.

Gloomy? No exit? Unduly pessimistic? Only to those who do not understand the 90 days of dying and rising with Christ, the annual journey of our church. To take on the discipline of Lent is to swallow false pride and leave personal fears and frights nailed to the cross. This is no regimen for the stoic. We submit to a period of purification and enlightenment to approach again the deliverance of the risen one. We dwell for 50 days on the glory that is ours. We personally appropriate that amazing grace in us, in our relationships, in our parishes. And it is all one movement to refresh us for the great sending of the Spirit.

The 90 days is the cause for the slight smile on the face of the vested Archbishop Romero assassinated at holy Mass. The dying-rising leads successful professionals to take enormous cuts in pay and give their lives to the mission of the church. In this Lent-Easter movement we find some parents struggling to discern whether to adopt another baby or join Maryknoll in Korea. This is the time when young women and men decide to leave the security of their families and assume the ministry of the word in action.

Lent and Easter, the springtime of a church owned exclusively by the Spirit, is the springboard for parish leadership to determine anew where to place its resources, how to budget its post-Pentecost activity, whether or not Matthew 25 has found a hearing here. Now is the crucial time to assess again the prospects of the seed, the word of God, and the soil under our noses where it has fallen. It is a time for communal and personal renewal that will stand up to the judgment of this world and render a judgment of its own.

Anyone who presumes to preach this powerful season knows a release of energy in the lives of the youngest, our elect and neophytes, as well as in those who may have burned out or become cynical. The word preached and prayed through these 90 days is the gift of the body of Christ to herself. This is the season of true self-nurture, of an intramural rebirth designed to take on the world outside the walls. It is a three month gestation for a nine month agenda. And the preacher is the exciter, the stimulator, the one who hones the two-edge sword.

Without this vision of these 90 days to Pentecost, the church will stay in the upper room focusing exclusively on the best way to set the table, prepare and distribute the food, teach our young their manners, and constantly rearrange the furniture. The gift of the Spirit is ample proof that domestic preoccupations are secondary to making the kingdom happen. We have figured out when and how to sing our songs in liturgy, how to bake our bread, and what series of texts best readies the kids for communion and confession. We have 20 years of experience with running parish council meetings and setting up committees, commissions and task forces. These matters take time, care and attention, as does personal growth in holiness and the whole range of self-nurturing ministries.

The reason for the in-house activities becomes clear only when we see those parishes that move outward to take on apathy and neglect, the plight of the least among us, or the forces that control and depress our neighborhoods and poison our young.

To complete the Lent-Eastertime vision we probably need to know toward what terminus our preaching is sending the faithful. Reread the Acts of the Apostles. Are we so sophisticated that we miss the message? The post-Pentecost church was so misunderstood by the world that it landed in jail, upside down on crosses and fed to the lions. Preaching sent them. I am in no rush to go to jail, but I do not underestimate the effects of preaching this Lent-Easter-Pentecost lectionary.

The "big 90" has to challenge the values we have gobbled up consciously and unconsciously from the world in which we live. Bad things happen to good people regardless of what T.V. and radio preachers say. There is nothing in the gospel that says the person who makes $100,000 per year is ten times better off in the sight of God than the one who makes $10,000. A country which sells more weapons than wheat to a trigger-happy world is not assured protection. A country which gives more favors to developers than to wholesome education and recreation for its young can expect to reap the whirlwind. Oh, there is a lot to examine during the "big 90," and we must do it within ourselves, our families, our parishes.

The occupational hazard of all organized religion is making itself the be-all and end-all of the energies of its adherents. John the Baptizer pointed beyond himself and the baptism he preached; he had his head handed to him. Before and after the Baptizer, a mark of fidelity has been cruel martyrdom. It is with us to this day. But the victory is real for those who walk with the church. It belongs not only to the living but to those who have died trying to move us back to the vision. "Everybody wants to go to heaven, but nobody wants to die," said the elderly Black who spent his life with the church. That is our lenten movement. And Eastertime is filled with these counsels: "You have nothing to fear. Peace."

The "big 90" encapsulates the dynamic of a faithful church: always a community of disciples becoming a community of apostles. Proclaim the fast, walk to Calvary, see the empty tomb, try the other side when you've caught nothing, be ready for a violent wind. The Spirit turns over tables and whips open the doors.

Taste the Lectionary and the Prayers

Ash Wednesday

The Ash Wednesday readings are important. It could be crucial to your parish to have your catechumens present. Refer to them so that those who attend only when we give things away (ashes, palms, etc.) know that more is going on here and feel the invitation to join. The enlightenment theme comes across in the alternative opening prayer. Use it to bring back a balance between enlightenment and purification. The agenda for Lent, inward and outward, is set: rend hearts, not garments; pray and fast; do good works.

If you have no catechumens, your parish ought to seriously consider why. Engage in prayer and fasting that your parish might be a light, that you may be seen as ambassadors for Christ, an Easter people.

First Sunday of Lent

If there is no one to elect on the First Sunday of Lent, avert from that and get at God's choice of *us*. The collect asks for help in understanding the Son's death and resurrection. Part of that is, of course, the Spirit's sending.

The prayer for the elect clearly describes the lenten mission of a parish with elect: "The chosen ones whom we lead with us to the Easter sacraments look to us for an example of Christian life." How are we doing individually and as a parish with temptations to absolute autonomy, to material goods, to playing God? Let's live on every utterance from the mouth of God.

Second Sunday of Lent

The gospel for the second Sunday, cycle A (Mt 17: 1-9), has Jesus imposing hands on Peter, James and John with an Easter message: "Get up, do not be afraid." It is not Pentecost; they are not yet to tell. But we go through Lent and Easter in order to tell. Tie it in.

The Scrutiny Sundays

The third lenten Sunday and the first scrutiny are loaded with anticipated postbaptismal catechesis. John's gospel is mystagogical catechesis, and the Spirit is alive and active. Authentic worshipers are in the Spirit. "One sows, another reaps" is as much for our generation as for the early church. Affirming Jesus as savior of the world is also a post-Easter and Pentecost experience.

An interesting slant to the exorcism prayers is their constant invocation of the messianic gifts. We have a host of cultural problems with exorcistic prayer but, by God, we need to name our demons and rely on a delivering power. The one who delivers us sets a sumptuous table, brings sight, heals wounds, strengthens the weak, restores health, finds the lost and saves the found. The messianic gifts are the reward for those who acknowledge their weaknesses and sins. Don't forget what this healing is for! Shalom is a condition for working to restore the world.

In the gospel for the fourth Sunday (cycle A) the man blind from birth is told to go and wash in the pool of Siloam, which means "one who has been *sent*." We are all getting ready to be washed—washed that we may be sent—sent into a people who are sharply divided by prophets.

The blind man suggests to the leadership of the organized religion that they might want to become Jesus' disciples. (Your parish is, in fact, working hard to become disciples in order to become apostles. The baptismal bath generates apostles. By the time of John's gospel you are something of a disciple *before* you are washed.) The seeing man gets thrown out for his faith.

And your parish is confronted with Jesus: "If you were blind, there would be no sin in that. But 'we see' you say and your sin remains." I submit that this is a crossover catechesis, a pre- *and* post-baptismal catechesis for those becoming disciples for the first time and for those who have been sent for a long time. Scrutinize yourself.

The last scrutiny Sunday begins in its alternative opening prayer with a cry for help "to embrace the world . . . that we may transform the darkness of its pain into the life and joy of Easter." Embracing the world is a Pentecost activity. Pain and sickness can be for God's glory, says Jesus, when he learns of Lazarus' illness. The healing visit to Lazarus has danger in it, a real risk: Thomas encourages the others to go along with Jesus to die with him.

After the touching description of tears and the picture of the cynics standing around, Jesus steps forth and commands, "Untie him and let him go free." That is an Easter-Pentecost declaration. There was very little freedom in that locked and secured upper room until the Spirit arrived. The prayer for the elect asks that they might bear witness to his resurrection, a truly Pentecost activity.

Eastertime

The Easter lectionary points so clearly to Pentecost. I have treated the mystagogical period in other sources (cf. "The Mystagogical Experience," *Christian Initiation Resources Reader*, New York: Sadlier, pp 54–69). Suffice it to say that all the readings from Acts and all of the gospels come from churches which have engaged the world. The chief reason we have this preaching and these remembrances preserved is to encourage your community of neophytes and believers to get on with it even, or especially, in the face of danger.

We get to the basis of ministry and mission when we touch the deepest parts of us that have been rescued by the passover of Christ. Preaching 50 days of the church at work in the context of the post-resurrection narratives and the last discourse is preamble to the communal celebration of being sent.

The homilies of Easter should create a challenging atmosphere for neophytes and the whole parish to come to grips with what they are willing to do individually and collectively after Pentecost. Lent should assess the impact of failures and useless burdens. Our preaching enlightens and purifies. Easter brings light and release. Our preaching should ready for sending.

John 14:12 crystallizes it for me (Fifth Sunday of Easter, cycle A): "The one who has faith in me will do the works I do, and greater far than these." What works are you planning? Where have your lenten reflections led you as individuals, families, parish? What have Easter, baptism, eucharist done to break you out of old ways and set you to work? Can we believe that we are to do more than Jesus did?

Spirit Sending

"Receive the Holy Spirit." "If you forgive sins, they are forgiven." To preach a parish into a ministry of reconciliation, of welcome and of peace is not easy. To extend that power and embrace the world with it scares most Catholics. The number of parishes who believe that they are called to make a difference is embarrassing. The suggestion that your parish ought seriously to confront injustices and inequities in your neighborhood in order to be faithful draws quizzical looks. However, the conviction of those who have worked with the gospel in the faith-sharing environment of a true catechumenate becomes clearer and clearer. We are in the business of baptizing, plunging folks into the real world.

Supported by one another and the variety of gifts that make up the body, we are sent to do a job. And the job is to take on powers and principalities bent on their own gain. In every parish worth its salt there are a few who look to the needs of others. To be sure, we are generous in countless second collections for missionary and self-help ventures. The Campaign for Human Development is a sign of that commitment. But the gospel clearly says to parishes who are listening, to parishes that are engaged in ongoing conversion, that the parish as a body has to take on its surroundings. We do well when we look beyond ourselves and are asked to give. The gospels, the neophytes, the preacher ask us to look around and beyond. Saul Alinsky and Dorothy Day have more to say to us about working our neighborhoods than we think. The test is not only in the amount of what we give but in what we do. Neophytes force us to *do*.

Let me be quite specific. The vision of Lent-Easter-Pentecost in the parish ought to take its shape from analysis of the injustices or troubles of its neighborhood, town, city or county, all the while keeping the international picture (questions of war and peace, of oppression and economic exploitation) in front of us because we are Catholic. The big picture may help us avoid another Catholic principle: we are responsible for all that happens in our boundaries. Rich parishes take care of poor parishes in the same diocese. Parishioners make sandwiches for downtown shelter and feeding programs. I believe our parishes would do more of that kind of thing if they began to work with the problems closer to home.

Most of our parishes are affluent, white and filled with families. Growing up in a society where drugs and alcohol are convenient diversions for the affluent and where little is done to assist teens is a major problem. Longevity is creating possibilities for serving our grandparents. The rate of divorce and of remarriage presents a host of opportunities for support. An uncertain economy and the migration of people from snow- to sun-belt offers the chance to parishes to organize employment placement and programs of welcome. The rush of immigration, legal and illegal, is testing liturgical and pastoral creativity. We have a hard time opening our doors to those who speak, pray and think differently than we. Disabilities afflict many of our members, and we often seem paralyzed in turning our desire to assist into concrete help.

From the richest of our parishes where finding good domestic help with transportation could provoke a deeper analysis of the conditions of our lower class to the poorest parishes caught in ghettos, the lectionary screams out: Save! Rendering to Caesar means keeping Caesar honest. How many of our parishes keep town councils honest, raise questions of the common good, work for legislation and community organizing. Rich and poor are called to that involvement in the world for all of the life issues which comprise our Catholic "seamless garment."

Our preaching, our parishes, our neophytes find the same two sources that give life: God's word in our time and place and the "big 90" days of Lent and Easter with neophytes bringing new energy to the work. They will push us out of our doors to re-create the face of our earth. And if we have no neophytes, our parishes can still work to the same end. They will attract inquirers when they show that the word is taking flesh in this parish. Preach the sending of the Spirit-filled people lest Lent, Easter and Pentecost be an intramural exercise repeated only for the sake of repetition. The liturgy of real people must lead to real action for charity, justice and peace, or the charade goes on.

Preaching in Eastertime: Reflections on the Nascent Church and Judaism

John T. Pawlikowski

The Easter cycle readings have a joyous tone about them. True, we learn of the fear and sufferings of Peter, Paul, and Stephen and other early church leaders as they attempt to express the new vision of divine reality they have experienced through Christ. But the dominant mood in the readings, and the mood that captures our spirits as we immerse ourselves in liturgical celebration during this season, is joyous and optimistic. Something new has dawned: people are beginning to grasp it, and increasing numbers, especially from the Gentile world, are associating themselves with the original community of Jesus' disciples.

The scriptural account of the church's infancy, related most comprehensively in the Acts of the Apostles which provides the first reading in the three cycles for all the Sundays of the Easter season (plus the feast of the Ascension), has the effect of rejuvenating the church's life today. These readings help us cut through centuries of ecclesiastical overlay. They return us, if only briefly, to the vitality and idealism of the initial gospel vision.

So most Christians would be rather surprised at the reaction of a rabbinic colleague of mine who attended a graduation Mass this Easter season. He has impeccable credentials in interreligious dialogue and a marked sensitivity for the constructive dimensions of the gospel. Yet he admitted to me that he would have left the Catholic church that morning after hearing the scripture readings if he had not feared offending the Catholic friends who had invited him. The strong implication that Jews were collectively responsible for the murder of the messiah, the deicide charge that has caused so much suffering and death for Jews throughout history, and John's talk of the disciples hiding for fear of "the Jews" were difficult words for this man who has always tried to combine a deep appreciation of his faith tradition with a genuine openness to Christianity.

On the basis of the readings he had heard, was it possible for the church to respect Judaism? Vatican Council II and statements by popes from John XXIII to John Paul II would seem to say yes. But he had to wonder what the congregants, especially the young graduates, would believe in this regard. Matters were made even worse by the presider, who in the prayers of the faithful thanked God for the faith "the Jews could not have." Had the conciliar declaration on the Jews' *Nostra Aetate*, the 1975 Vatican guidelines and a series of guidelines from the American bishops made any impact? Or was the typical Catholic congregation's attitude towards Jews and Judaism still shaped by the image of Jews as "rejectionists," and dangerous ones at that, rather than as a people whose faithfulness to the word of God remains unbending? In the recent book, *The Body of Faith*, the ecumenical Jewish scholar Michael Wyschograd raises this question quite directly: Why is it that Christians focus only on the moments of Israel's unfaithfulness and almost never at all on the moments of deep and uncompromising faithfulness?

A Real Tension

We need to take my rabbinic friend's troubled reaction to one part of the Easter cycle very seriously in light of the call for increased Christian appreciation of Judaism and improved Christian-Jewish relations by Vatican Council II and recent popes. For this rabbi was in fact raising questions about attitudes that permeate the scripture selections in the three cycles of Easter readings—attitudes which have a pronounced anti-Judaic potential.

And this is the nub of the problem of conveying a positive sense of Judaism in liturgy, catechetics or theology. Anti-Judaic statements that are easily transformed into outright anti-Semitism are found at the core of the Christian proclamation. The problem will not be resolved simply by eliminating a few scripture passages or prayers from liturgical use. It always amazes me that people in the church think the dilemma of anti-Judaism and the scriptures is over and done with, that the problem was totally resolved by the council and the actions of Pope John XXIII when he struck the term "perfidious Jews" from the Good Friday liturgy. The readings of the Easter cycles and my rabbinic colleague's reaction to one part of them should convince us otherwise.

What then, are the principal sources of tension for the contemporary Christian-Jewish encounter arising out of the Eastertime Sunday readings? The first is the overriding impression that the Jews put Jesus to death because he was challenging the superficiality of their faith. On the Third Sunday of Easter (cycle A) we hear Peter charge the "men of Israel" with using "pagans to crucify and kill" Jesus after he had proven himself as one sent by God. The tenor of the argument is much the same in the B cycle selection for the same Sunday. Peter bluntly blames the people (Jews by implication) for the failure of Pilate to release Jesus: "You disowned the Holy and Just One and preferred instead to be granted the release of a murderer. You put to death the author of life." Similar thoughts about Jewish responsibility for the crucifixion occur on the Fourth Sunday of Easter (cycles A and B).

Understanding the Full Context

These texts easily reinforce an anti-Judaic interpretation of the Christian message. We should not pretend otherwise. Hence, these texts need to be met head-on by the homilist. Two points are crucial here for interpreting the church-synagogue relationship within the New Testament. The first is setting such statements within their *original social context* to the extent that contemporary scholarship can recreate that. The second is placing various New Testament texts dealing with the same subject matter side-by-side so that an *overall assessment* can be made of the thrust of an argument. In other words, when the New Testament exhibits differing emphases with respect to the same issue, no one text should be proclaimed to the congregation as *the* New Testament viewpoint.

The Peter-statements in Acts of Jewish responsibility for the death of Jesus need to be subjected to the application of both principles. The social context is crucial. Peter is still speaking from within the larger Jewish community to people who look upon themselves as faithful Jews. The first reading from Acts 2, used in the A cycle for the Second Sunday of Easter, reports that the followers of Jesus "went to the Temple area together every day, while in their homes they broke bread."

So it seems that for Peter's Jerusalem community the Jewish tradition remained vital to their faith expression despite their experience of a renewed vision in Jesus. Peter believed that what Jesus had given his disciples would enhance rather than obliterate the Torah system that had provided meaning and direction for their lives. In sharing the enthusiasm for the new vision in Christ, Peter obviously became frustrated when the Jewish leadership and many of the people seemed unwilling to be touched by the joy and vitality the vision had added to the essentially Jewish faith life of the apostolic church. Frustration born out of enthusiasm for a new vision often leads to exaggerated charges. Some of that is likely operative in Acts. After weighing the evidence regarding Jewish responsibility for Jesus' death found in the relevant New Testament books, biblical scholars today have a strong consensus that at best a select number of Jewish leaders collaborated with the Roman imperial government in the decision to execute. And many of these Jewish leaders were not highly regarded within Jewish circles of the time and were looked upon as exploiters of their own people for personal gain.

What we have in Acts may be a case of youthful enthusiasm in the midst of identity development which led to the early Christian community's extension of blame beyond the actual facts of the case. It must also be said that it is not fully clear whom Peter is blaming in some of the passages. In certain cases the accusation seems to be directed against leaders, in others against the people-at-large. Nor can we discount the possibility that the Peter-speeches reflect the spirit of competition for converts with Judaism and growing institutional estrangement that were prevalent at the time of the composition of Acts (70 A.D.) or even later. We may be dealing here with a reflection of the social context of the Jewish-Christian relationship in the latter part of the first century more than with the actual attitudes of the post-Easter Jerusalem church.

Homilists will certainly want to convey the spirit and enthusiasm of the early church. But in so doing the responsibility to place

Peter's remarks in their full context is part of the reconciliation between Jews and Christians to which we have been summoned by both John XXIII and John Paul II.

The Faithful Jews

A related concern which emerges from the Easter cycle readings is the depiction of Jews exclusively as obstructionists, what many today call nay-sayers, with respect to the gospel. The reading from John used each year on the Second Sunday of Easter and repeated every Pentecost describes the disciples hiding in fear of "the Jews." Without doubt this leaves a negative image with hearers of the word in our time. The same holds for the story of the dismissal of the apostles by the Sanhedrin and the order "not to speak again about the name of Jesus" from the Acts selection for the Third Sunday of Easter (C cycle). See also the first reading for the Fourth Sunday of Easter (C cycle), which speaks of the expulsion of Paul and Barnabas from Antioch, and the fifth Sunday in cycle B which mentions the attack on Paul by the Greek-speaking Jews.

Again the social context becomes important in any homiletic interpretation of these texts. In John's gospel we come face-to-face with the thorny problem of his generalized use of "the Jews" rather than referring, as the other gospels do, to specific Jewish groups. This problem is not totally resolved in scholarly circles. And there may be no one alternative term applicable to the Johannine use of "the Jews." But in this selection it appears that the Jewish leadership, probably those connected with the temple administration, were the only ones intended.

As for the other passages, some of the points made earlier about the murder-of-the-Messiah statements apply as well. Our sympathies as Christian worshipers will certainly remain in large measure with Paul and the apostles. Some of the people who opposed them were undoubtedly bent on safeguarding their own interests, but that is not the full story. As we Christians share anew each Easter season the vision of Christ proclaimed by the apostles, we must recognize that some of the Jewish leaders who opposed them may not have been mere obstructionists protecting their own flank. Rather, they may have been gravely concerned that the manner of proclamation and the decisions of the early church with respect to the place of the Jewish tradition might undermine the religious vision of the Hebrew Scriptures (which, we know, was central for Jesus himself). They may likewise have concluded that some of the enthusiastic announcements about the presence of the final kingdom may have been dangerously premature, despite a growing awareness of the imminence of the kingdom in rabbinic circles. In this area the church had to draw back somewhat by the end of the first century.

As we reflect on the significance of these passages today, two attitudes need to emerge. First is the clear recognition and proclamation that the Jewish "no" to Jesus may not simply have been hardheaded rejection but an attempt to preserve the religious roots of the gospel in the Jewish tradition (which the church has not done all that well over the centuries), and to warn us of the abuses associated with some Christological affirmations, especially excessively individualistic interpretations of the Christ-event's significance for human salvation which have so frequently crept into the church's spirituality and liturgy.

The second attitude is that conveyed in the remarkable paper presented by Professor Tomaso Federici, a Roman biblical scholar, at an international meeting of Catholics and Jews in 1978 cosponsored by the Vatican. In that paper Professor Federici argued that dialogue between Christians and Jews must now become the norm for carrying out the "witness" mandate given to us in the Matthew selection used in all cycles for the feast of the Ascension. In the dialogue we as Christians will certainly wish in an appropriate manner to share the enthusiasm generated within us through the hearing of the church's birth. But we will also recognize that in the struggle to establish its distinct identity, in the separation of church and synagogue, Christianity may have seriously eroded, if not totally lost, a precious legacy—the tradition of the Hebrew Scriptures and the reflections upon them by subsequent generations of Jewish religious teachers. Such a wholesale discarding of the Jewish tradition was definitely not in the mind of Jesus as he proclaimed his message. It would have been impossible for Jesus to give us the word he did if he had not been able to draw upon the prophets and the Torah and the further developments in Judaism associated with the Pharisaic revolution.

A gospel without its Jewish base is a truncated form of Jesus' message. This is what the Jewish "no" to Jesus, despite its awkwardness and its difficulty for the apostles at the time, has preserved for Christians today. Thus, in the dialogue, we Christians also need to encounter Jewish faith expression. We do not enter the contemporary dialogue with Jews simply as "givers," but also as "receivers." This is a thrust that must be conveyed in the proclamation of the word throughout the Easter season. In this regard it is unfortunate that the Hebrew Scriptures are not used at all during the Easter cycles. Perhaps this will be corrected one day. For it leaves the impression that the Hebrew Scriptures have no part in this positive expression of the fundamentals of our faith life as Christians. It blocks our ability to recognize, for example, that the reality of the Spirit that we proclaim so prominently during this season is a profoundly Jewish reality spoken of in the book of Joel and elsewhere.

Continuity with Jewish Roots

In concluding this examination of the anti-Semitic potential in the Easter cycle readings mention needs to be made of the narrative of the Council of Jerusalem found in the Acts reading on the Sixth Sunday of Easter (C cycle). The results of the Council—nonmaintenance of Jewish practices such as circumcision for new converts to the church—had a profound effect on Christianity's future orientation. Our impulse as Christians is to identify with Paul's defense of "freedom" on this question while looking upon the Jerusalem church led by Peter and James as unnecessarily restricted in its outlook. Perhaps the latter were such. But before we applaud Paul's victory at the council too loudly we ought at least consider the side of Peter and James. Though they, too, were concerned about the forging of a new identity for the young and growing church, they rightly believed that deep ties with the Jewish tradition should remain, for these were crucial for Jesus. They no doubt understood how profoundly the Jewish tradition had shaped his own thinking from their personal association with his ministry. To abruptly sever the church's Jewish roots risked seriously emasculating the gospel. Reluctantly they went along with Paul, concluding that circumcision and similar practices were not the best way to accomplish this goal.

But Peter's and James' worst fears were frequently realized in subsequent centuries. Paul may have been right in setting Christianity on a new course. But Peter and James were also correct in insisting on the continuation of ties with the Jewish tradition. It is a shame that the epistle of James is not read in the Sunday liturgy during the Easter cycles (though it is used on weekdays and in the liturgy of the hours), for its thoroughly Jewish perspective can counteract the danger of a totally separatist mentality with respect to Judaism that can result from listening to the Council of Jerusalem report.

The Easter season is certainly a time of joy and vitality. The homilist needs to make that spirit come alive in reflections on the proclaimed word. But there is need as well to remind the congregation continually that the narrative of the young church's struggle for identity must be set in the context of the whole New Testament, including the pervasive Jewish spirit of Jesus' teachings as reported in the gospels and Paul's mature observations (Romans 9–11) about the ongoing validity of Judaism.

Contributors

Eleanor Bernstein, CSJ is director of the Center for Pastoral Liturgy at the University of Notre Dame. She holds master's degrees in theology and in liturgical studies.

John Buscemi, a priest of the diocese of Madison, Wisconsin, holds a degree in fine arts from the University of Wisconsin, Madison. He is a liturgical consultant for the building and renovation of churches.

Cheryl Dieter is a theological librarian at the Jesuit-Krauss-McCormick Library in Chicago. She also works as music director for Bethlehem Lutheran Church in Chesterton, Indiana.

Richard N. Fragomeni is currently a doctoral student at Catholic University. He is a priest of the diocese of Albany, where he was director of the diocesan liturgy center. He is on the board of the North American Forum on the Catechumenate.

Brian L. Helge is an ordained pastor in the Lutheran Church of America.

Gabe Huck, director of Liturgy Training Publications, is widely known for his writing on the keeping of the seasons. He is the author of *The Three Days: Parish Prayer in the Paschal Triduum* (LTP).

Raymond B. Kemp, priest of the archdiocese of Washington, serves his diocese as secretary for parish life and worship. He writes and speaks frequently on the development of the RCIA.

Eugene LaVerdiere, SSS, a noted scripture scholar and teacher, is currently editor of *Emmanuel Magazine.*

John T. Pawlikowski, OSM, is a member of the Catholic Bishops' Secretariat for Catholic-Jewish Relations and is on the faculty of Catholic Theological Union in Chicago.

JoAnne Timmerman, OP, is a musician and liturgist on the staff of St. Dominic Parish in Denver. She did her liturgical studies at St. John's University in Collegeville, Minnesota.